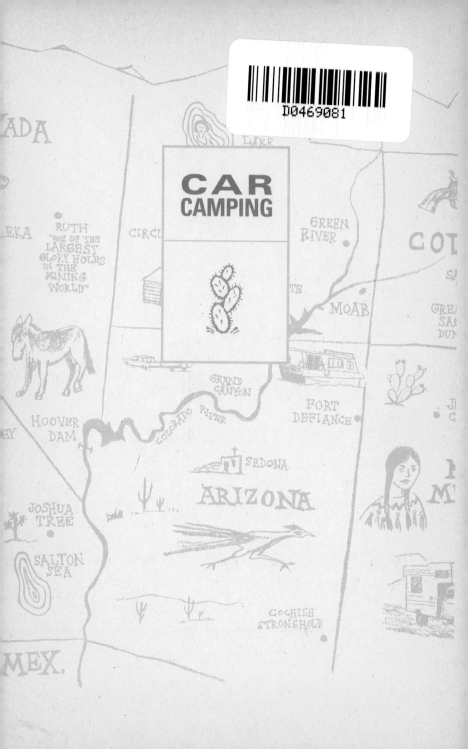

CAR
CAMPING

CAR CAMPING

THE BOOK OF DESERT ADVENTURES

MARK SUNDEEN

WITH ARTISTIC DRAWINGS BY ERIK R. BLUHM

Quill
An Imprint of
HarperCollins*Publishers*

HarperCollins books may be purchased for educational, business, or sales promotional use. For information please write: Special Markets Department, HarperCollins Publishers Inc., 10 East 53rd Street, New York, NY 10022.

FIRST EDITION

Designed by Deborah Kerner

Library of Congress Cataloging-in-Publication Data has been applied for.

ISBN 0-688-17460-4

00 01 02 03 04 RRD 10 9 8 7 6 5 4 3 2 1

Author's Note

Dear Shopper,

This book is about camping and I knew you would not pay twenty-five dollars for it. For that kind of money you could get literature. You could get a glossy hardcover with the author on the back making a very smart face.

That's not how I wanted this book. I personally think that literature is overpriced, and I won't buy it. All you get is a bunch of words. I wanted *Car Camping* to be unlike literature in two ways. I wanted it cheap and I wanted it true.

The first one was easy: I made it a paperback. You will see that I did not include a lot of fancy words or expensive ideas. To make sure that you get your money's worth, I added some maps, drawings, and pictures at no extra cost.

I tried hard to keep it a true book. Most of these chapters came out in *Great God Pan* magazine between 1993 and 2000 in an adventure column called "Car Camping: A Guide to Recreation in the Western U.S." The editor there let me write anything as long as it was true, and that's what I did. But when

I went to turn the stories into a book, the book people said instead of having a bunch of separate little adventures could I please just make it one big story. I said fine, but I might have to make some stuff up to plug up the gaps. This book is the result. I hope you will forgive me for the fake parts.

One more thing. I have changed the names of some of the places because the people who live there don't want any more visitors. Be careful. If you follow my directions you will never get where you want to go.

—MARK SUNDEEN
Moab, Utah

Contents

The sweating, dusty, desolate, sun-raddled wastes, the ill-built, creaking buildings, the lost, vacant people and their pointless actions—this was a proper and salutary antidote to the sentimentalized desert of so many well-meaning ecological desert lovers, because this was an equally true version of the American desert as it really is, all too often. When you turn from contemplating the deep satisfactions of the sunset, or from marveling at the stripes of morning mist across the Little Cowhole Mountain, what assaults your eyes on the other side of the road or parking lot is a landscape of moral anorexia, collapsed Chevrolets, and mountains of beer cans, a landscape tolerable only through a haze of barbiturate fumes.

—REYNER BANHAM,
Scenes in America Deserta

With other men, perhaps, such things would not have been inducements; but as for me, I am tormented with an everlasting itch for things remote.

—HERMAN MELVILLE,
Moby-Dick

*I keep running from life
but I can't get away.*

—MERLE HAGGARD

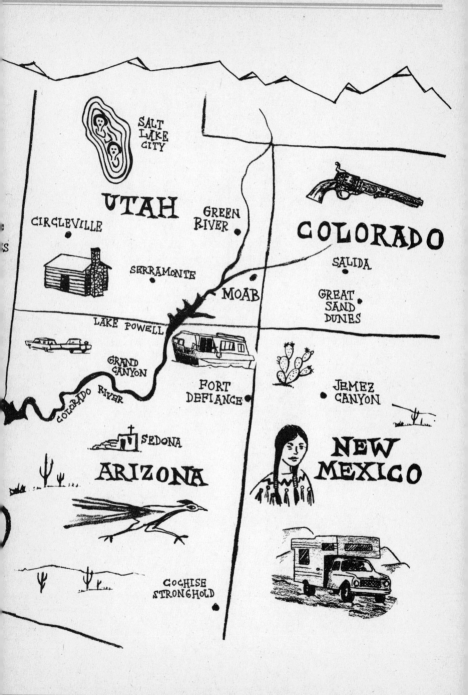

PART
ONE

A Money Town

SEDONA, ARIZONA

There's nothing wrong with the desert. You can live wherever you want. My cousin Donny Brown lived a summer in Bullhead City, where if you fell on the sidewalk you'd get a burn, and he said that was fine.

For that matter there's nothing wrong with anything somebody else does. I say let them. Look at all the people moving to the desert to write poems or dig for gemstones or build a house out of mud and twigs. If anyone asks, they say it's great and it's very spiritual and they're getting in touch with the Earth. That's fine with me.

Or what about my Aunt Rachel? Two years ago when she found out she might be part Indian, she disappeared with a man in his big pickup truck. There was no word. Then one day she called her son Donny Brown and said she was finally living her life's dream. She and her new husband had settled on a black farm near Prescott, Arizona.

I asked Donny Brown what a black farm was.

"You know, they painted the barn and stable black, and the

fences. They have a black cow, black roosters, a black billy goat, stuff like that. Some black cats."

The reason Aunt Rachel left in the first place was finding out about her father. She and my mom had never known him. All they knew was that he was adopted and that he died in a car wreck in 1942. But when my grandmother was on her deathbed she told them the whole story. Turned out my grandfather's real mother was a prostitute in Tucson who'd been seen on the Fort Apache reservation. He was so ashamed of possibly being an Indian that he made my grandmother promise never to tell anyone.

I didn't see what was to be ashamed of. When my cousins and I found out we might be Indian we thought it was sort of cool. People said that now we might get a better job. For a while when I looked in the mirror I thought I saw a little bit of red, but then I realized that even if I was one part Indian I was still seven parts white. I was white. The story about the Apache reservation didn't matter. I'd been white for twenty years and it was too late to learn how to be an Indian. And besides, I thought the only job I could get out of it was in a casino, and I'm terrible at cards.

But Aunt Rachel was changed. She said she'd always felt like an Indian, known it inside, and the news just confirmed her gut instinct. She left L.A. and wasn't heard from for two years. Now she called Donny Brown and told him she was more in touch with the Earth than she'd ever been with anything.

"Does she know how to farm?" I asked him.

"That's the thing," he said. "She invited me out there because she says I have a green thumb. They want to grow some black flowers."

There were three of us cousins traveling to Arizona in the station wagon. One was Donny Brown, one was Shapiro Brown, one was me. They were going to see their mother and Donny said I could come too if I drove my car. I always did what he told me because it always turned into an adventure.

Donny Brown was my favorite person. He was six and a half feet tall and an expert camper. Over the years he had impressed and even silenced me with the way he lashed bicycles to the bumper or pitched tarps in a hail shower. He was the height I wanted to be, and I always liked the way he walked into a room thin and windblown and hungry. It seemed like he'd been out in a cold storm while everyone else had just been lazy on the couch.

Everything always went his way. Now Donny Brown had a good job as a rock singer and a pretty wife who paid the mortgage, and I loved everything about him, including his wife, especially his wife. I had also gone on dates with two of his ex-girlfriends. If he ever found out about it he never said so.

Shapiro was a novice camper and I wasn't much better. While Donny Brown was a success, his brother and I were failures. We were both housepainters still living at home. Either of us would have dropped the other in a minute to spend a day with Donny Brown.

We had left L.A. and picked up Donny in San Francisco, and planned to exit California through Death Valley, then make our way through Arizona. Donny Brown was vague about where Aunt Rachel lived, but I guessed we could find out later.

He said we should go to Sedona on the way. I had never heard of it and neither had Shapiro, but we all agreed it made for a good destination. Later we found out that Donny Brown didn't know where it was or what was there or why he wanted to go there. Maybe he had meant to say Sonoma or Salida or any other town. But that was all right, because driving over the Sierras at six A.M. it sounded better to say we were going to Sedona than to say we were going to look for a black farm or to say we didn't know where we were going at all.

Nothing happens in Death Valley and there's nothing to do. I liked it. From the minute we topped Panamint Pass and coasted toward the valley floor, everything was perfectly still. The wind blew and blew with no result. The valley was enclosed by brown, slumped mountains and littered with dark chunks of rock, and just sat there like a picture of itself.

Shapiro and Donny Brown and I climbed the Panamint Sand Dunes, smoked a cigarette, then somersaulted down. It was early April and not very hot. We walked out on the endless salt flats behind Badwater and stood for half an hour above the rocks at Zabriske Point. I thought something bold and dramatic might happen if I waited long enough.

We got in the car and drove to Hoover Dam.

In the desert, things are enormous and you can get on them. That's why people like it there. We reached Hoover Dam late at night and leaned far over the concrete restraint and spat. The spittle whipped in the wind and floated down the dizzying gorge. We drove two days. At night we slept in flat areas off the highway and cooked hot dogs on a fire in the gravel. We didn't talk to anyone.

We got to Cape Royal at the Grand Canyon where a sharp

finger of rock protruded far into the gorge. We walked along the nature trail sipping beer. Out there the air was thin and cool and a pleasant breeze blew. We squatted over the rim and crapped and watched them sail away.

There was a lot to see down in the canyon, but we were already tired. We turned around. Down the footpath came a troop of schoolchildren. The boys wore crisp jeans and neat plaid shirts. The girls wore blue jeans underneath plaid dresses. We stepped off the trail to let them pass, then from an observation point watched them file onto the cape, look at the vista, snap photographs, and file off. Some were holding hands.

We walked to the parking lot. A minute later the children clambered by and boarded a long yellow bus. None looked at us. The chaperone conducted a count, and they drove off.

Their outing to Grand Canyon had been sound, sensible, and as far as I could tell, entirely successful. Shapiro asked what to do with the empties and I said crush them and put them back in the cooler. You could get five cents apiece at the store. Donny Brown covered his face with his hands and cried very quietly.

We didn't talk. I had never seen him cry before. Now our car trip wasn't as fun as I'd hoped it would be. I looked out the window and Shapiro looked at a map and Donny Brown drove the car fast. At the first gas station, I bought another sixpack while Donny Brown telephoned his wife in California. She said she didn't want to talk with him and hung up. He called back but she wouldn't answer. Shapiro asked the man behind the counter which way we needed to go.

The man pointed at a map.

"It's a money town, Sedona."

"It's not so far from Prescott," Shapiro said.

"Bunch of jerk-offs in Prescott, too," he said. "Californians."

We crossed the Colorado River at Marble Canyon and drove south. Black clouds hovered on the plateau. Donny Brown made us stop again to use the payphone. He let it ring twenty-five times.

"I bet she's with Jack Hammond," Donny told us. "I bet they're going to Half Moon Bay together. Hey, Shapiro, do you know Jack Hammond?"

I wished there was something to do besides drive but there wasn't, so we kept going. Donny Brown struggled to keep his mind off his wife and Shapiro struggled to open a can of tamales with a Swiss Army knife. Both were dull and dark. I felt fine but kept it to myself so they wouldn't think I was an ass.

I didn't know what to do. I kept expecting Donny Brown to snap out of it and make something exciting happen, but he just sat there in the passenger seat drinking beer. Sure he was upset, but if she were my wife, I'd be back there with her and not driving all over the desert in a station wagon. It was his own fault for leaving, is what I thought.

The rainclouds broke open in Flagstaff, then blew past as we wound down Oak Creek Canyon. Streams of rainwater ran out of the woods and across the asphalt. We entered Sedona town limits.

"It's a money town," said Shapiro.

"Jack Hammond is a cock," said Donny Brown.

Sedona was a strip of brightly painted storefronts built to look like an Old West mining town. Inside the stores they sold paperweights, hats with feathers, and candy that came in a box instead of a wrapper. It was like Knotts Berry Farm without the rides.

It was a little past four. Luckily there was a tavern. We bought a pack of cigarettes and went inside and after a few rounds of Löwenbräu we got settled. The bar was cozy and dark and just right, which was a good thing. We were about to spend eight hours in there. Donny Brown came back from the pay phone and said he'd reached his stepfather.

"Did you get directions?" I asked.

"He said it's about a hundred miles from here. He's gonna come meet us."

"What about your mom?"

"She's sick in bed and couldn't come to the phone. That's what he said, anyway."

We drank beer and whiskey for four hours. When six college girls filed in and took over a table I imagined how they would lure me into their dormitory. My cousins fell mute and stared and drank steadily. Hours later some boys with sun visors and short pants entered the bar and befriended the girls. We turned our backs and sent for more liquor. Donny Brown cried for a little while. The bartender brought out free appetizers and we ate the cheese plate and the decorative melon.

Then the three of us started to talk, me and Shapiro and Donny. We said how much we liked each other. We remembered the way we used to set up a tent in my backyard and throw berries at cars and later on invite girls to sneak over. It felt good. We talked some more. We were starting to talk about how glad we were to be related when a man who was a bit older than us slid into the booth.

"You must be the dude I'm looking for," he said to Donny Brown. "I've seen your picture. I'm the Ricker."

We all shook his hand and said our names. He was wearing

a golf shirt, crisp pleated jeans and cowboy boots. He had an excellent suntan. Shapiro asked how far a drive it was to the black farm, and the Ricker said he had a motel room upcanyon for all of us and wanted to have a good time.

"I've got a thousand dollars in my pocket," he said. He held up his wallet and thumbed through the bills. The Ricker was not a liar.

"Beers all around!" he shouted.

While we drank he told us about the truck he drove, explained the real estate appraisal business, whispered some strategies for keeping the wetbacks out of a good neighborhood, and announced that he could get a thirty-year at seven and a quarter.

"Recession be damned," he said. "Arizona is still a hot buy." We nodded.

"You dudes look like hell," he said. "How long you been on the road?"

"We're having a fair trip," I said.

He pointed to a man and a woman on the dance floor. I realized then that there was loud music and many people in the tavern. The woman wore cowboy boots and cutoff blue jeans and she let the man put his hands all over her body.

"That's my buddy Bri," said the Ricker. "We're taking the chick back to the hotel room. You dudes want to party on her?"

We all said we did. I don't remember the exact sequence of what happened next. We drank some more and finished the cigarettes. I went to the bathroom more than once and then we three were out in the parking lot. Now we were really going to party. But then Donny Brown said to hell with it, we oughta bolt straight back to California. I think what he meant was he

wanted to get back with his wife, but what he said was, "Let's
get the hell out of this money town," and I said, "Yeah, fuck it."

But Shapiro said he was going to stay. He said he didn't care
about the chick but he wanted to see his mom.

We stood there and looked at each other. Lightning flashed.

A shiny diesel crewcab rumbled up. Inside, the chick sat
between the Ricker and his buddy Bri. Shapiro hauled his bag
out of the station wagon and heaved it into the truck bed. He
said bye and got in.

"You dudes are missing out," said the Ricker. He gunned it
and kicked up gravel as he roared off.

We started to drive. Me and Donny Brown. We were headed
west. It rained for a long time and we turned up the radio, and
when it stopped raining we turned it down. In Jerome people
spilled out of a saloon and into the street. We drove along,
nothing on the road but the beams of our own headlights.

"I'm a bad man," said Donny Brown. "I feel different now."

By the time we reached Prescott it was the middle of the
night. Most of the lights were out. I said to Donny that
Shapiro must really miss his mom and he said some people are
weak like that, and he drove on, and by the time we laid our
sleeping bags out on the dewy roadside buffalo grass we were
back in California.

CHAPTER 2

Down Here
in the Hobbit Hole

JOSHUA TREE, CALIFORNIA

My first adventure was to Joshua Tree when I was fifteen. Donny Brown taught me to rockclimb. He showed me which knots to tie, how to wedge a chock in a crack then pop it out with a screwdriver, and how to smear the soles of my boots on the rock so that I could balance without my hands. We were the same age, but he was the one who knew what to do.

One night it snowed. Young Tom and Alfy the cobbler, who lived out there, walked into our camp and stood by the fire with a pot of hot soup to share. The snow didn't stop so we all crowded into a small foreign station wagon that smelled bad and passed around the soup.

When we got out of the car, the sky was clear. Most of the snow had melted and the ground was glowing beneath the round moon. The rocks were like lumps of ice cream starting to melt.

We sprinted across the desert and leapt over chollas and yuccas and quartzite boulders. We could run forever. I looked over at my cousin Donny Brown. He was smiling. He was not looking at me.

"I didn't know how long we could go driving around like this."

We ran faster.

Donny Brown was a screen. He crossed the landscape like a fishnet through a clear pond. He gulped up clusters of stars and they danced out the back of his head.

I wanted to be him, for life to rush through me as fast as it arrived, not caught up on thoughts or thinking. That's the only thing I've really wanted.

Donny Brown and I rested somewhere in the Real Hidden Valley. I have no theories about what became of the other people. We lay on the rocks like we were on the moon. We were the age when things could look like that.

Then I heard noises. Short, high-pitched chirps. They were sharp and hollow and went on for a while and wove strange melodies. I couldn't tell where the music came from or what was making it. It couldn't be a bird. I lay there and listened and I liked it. After a long time it stopped.

"What do you think was making that sound?" I said out loud.

Donny answered from somewhere behind me. "Which one?"

"That one like a bird."

"What did you think it was?"

"I don't know."

"That was me," he said. "I was singing."

We were much older now. We were adults. We had just driven from Arizona to California.

When we woke up in the buffalo grass, it was already afternoon. My head hurt. By the time we got some food and started driving, it was dusk. We passed Joshua Tree National Monument on Interstate 10. This was back before it became a Park. It was dark by the time we got to Palm Springs, and the electric signs were lit up on the avenue. There was a pool hall. We shot some games and drank a pitcher.

The only one in there besides us was the bartender. Donny Brown asked if there were any girls in town and the bartender nodded. We drove down the strip to the Pink Lady.

There was no cover so I could afford a bottle of Miller. It was $3.75. I paid with a five and got change and tucked the bill in the girl's panties when she came down off the stage. She told me her name was Tiffany.

When she turned away, I still had a quarter in my hand and didn't know what to do with it. I threw it on the floor.

Donny Brown went to the payphone and when he came back I could tell his wife hadn't answered. He sat down and we tipped back the beer bottles. Donny took a pill. He didn't say what it was. I think he thought I didn't notice.

"From here on out," he said, "I'm living in the Right Now."

"In the what what?"

"The Right Now," he said. "Forget about the past and the future. That's how we live, the Right Now. We do what we need to as the situation arises. It's in our blood."

Then he said I wasn't supposed to know about this but his mom had told him some more stuff about our grandfather. He was a bad man, she had said. He didn't die in a car accident like they'd always told us. Actually he'd gone AWOL from Camp Pendleton and held up a gas station in Flagstaff, Arizona. He shot the attendant in the leg and made off with two thousand dollars from the cash drawer. He was last seen heading north into the canyons, but the state police and park service couldn't find him. He just vanished. He was never seen again.

I could tell that I was supposed to feel different now that I was a bad man, but I felt the same as always. Donny Brown was very serious about the story he had told me and I didn't want to tell him that my mom had already told me the same one, except that in her version my grandfather only made off with two hundred forty dollars instead of two thousand. Also in my mom's version, my grandfather called home six months after the robbery and asked my grandmother to take him back. She said go to hell, and later that year he got drunk and stumbled out in front of a truck and died in a car wreck after all.

"I'm a bad man," said Donny Brown. "You too. Nothing we can do about it. We're bad men living in the Right Now."

The song ended and I clapped. Then I thought maybe I shouldn't have clapped because the song and the dance were already in the past, not in the Right Now. Donny Brown wasn't clapping.

"Let's go have an adventure," he said. "Let's go to Joshua Tree."

Another girl got up to dance and we drank the beer.

There we sat, me and my cousin Donny Brown at age twenty-two in the Pink Lady in Palm Springs wondering about the grandfather we'd never met and trying to have an adventure while a girl lay on her back in underpants and opened and shut her legs in time to "Hotel California."

We got on Highway 62 and climbed up into the high desert toward Joshua Tree, passing back and forth a bottle of Ten High. I watched Donny Brown drive the car. The oncoming headlights sifted through him.

He was in the Right Now, but I was not. I was usually somewhere else besides where I was. I've always been like that. If you asked me right now how I was or who I was I couldn't tell you, but I could tell you a lot of other things. I could tell you that more than one hundred years ago Bill and Jim McHaney came out from Missouri in a covered wagon with their parents and grazed cattle right near here at the Twentynine Palms Oasis. It was good range if you could find enough water. I knew that Johnny Lang drove in a herd and that C. O. Barker came over from Banning. Barker built a dam in the Wonderland of Rocks, and it's still there, a concrete wedge and a pond of stagnant rainwater that's green and lush where everything around is desert.

Once I fell in to my waist and it was slimy.

I could also tell you that Johnny Lang claimed the Lost Horse Gold Mine in what became the Monument. For two years he made three thousand dollars a day, but never got rich. He sent his share to his dance-hall wife in Tombstone, and when he sold his claim she divorced him. Thirty years later he turned up dead in the road not five miles from Lost Horse.

Bill and Jim McHaney staked out the Desert Queen. Now the shafts are sealed with iron bars and there's nothing to see. But if you know where to look, you can still find open tunnels. Their cabin is tucked under a cliff, with neat masonry walls of square flat stones and no mortar. There are cups and forks and barrels and a window made of real glass. The brothers lived there and dug and when the ore ran thin lost their claim to the bank. Bill prospected in the desert for thirty-six more years and Jim was sent to the penitentiary for counterfeiting. You can still see the hole they dug and the dirt they carried out.

These were the things I thought about as we wound through the desert. The entrance booth was closed so we drove on through. Donny cut the headlights. There was a big moon up and the skeleton shadows of the Joshua trees lay down on the road.

Hidden Valley Campground was the first legal place to stay. There were two camp loops, no water, no electricity, no flush toilets. It was free. We found a site up against the rock wall called the Blob. It was my favorite site because in the rock 100 feet above the picnic table was the Space Station, a cave big enough that one Halloween I'd seen it fit six people, a dome tent, a fiery jack-o'-lantern, and a medium-size house dog called Bud.

"Let's climb up there," said Donny Brown.

He led me from the car around the corner of the Blob to a steep rock ramp. He'd been this way before, but I hadn't. The climbing wasn't too hard except that it was cold and we were drunk and didn't have the right shoes on. The ledge narrowed into a little lip way up off the ground. Below was a little window in the rock.

Donny went first, keeping his heels down. I climbed down and slid through the window. We were in the Space Station. Looking over the campground we saw fires burning and fancy jeeps parked everywhere. The rock was cold beneath me.

Next, Donny Brown wanted to go to the Great Chasm.

The Great Chasm is a secret entrance into the Real Hidden Valley, which is just across the road from camp. It's a flat basin surrounded by jumbles of rock where seventy-five years ago Jim and Bill McHaney hid the cattle they stole. We climbed down from the Space Station and started walking. Alfy the cobbler and Young Tom had led us through the chasm when we were sixteen. They didn't let us bring flashlights.

Back then Hidden Valley Campground was all bums and dirtbags. Alfy lived in a cave in Site 12 and made money repairing and resoling climbing boots. I remember watching him one morning cook a tin cup of green beans and butter on the fire. Young Tom was only a couple years older than us. He always said he'd been an honor student at Redondo High School till he dropped out, but all I ever saw him do was smoke dope and set gas fires.

The Tucker brothers lived there too. They were scary and I thought that if they weren't rockclimbers they would be on skid row or in jail. They had first names but we called them both Tucker. They made runs to Mexico and brought back cheap climbing rubber and grocery bags of weed. Tucker gave me my first pair of climbing boots with soles he'd put on himself. They smelled so bad that my mom made me keep them outside. The sole peeled off. Eventually the Tuckers punched Alfy in the head because he'd won all the customers.

I remembered once seeing the third Tucker. His brothers

had taken him out of a hospital in L.A. where he'd been since he fell eighty feet in Yosemite Valley. He was slumped in a wheelchair beside the campfire with shiny silver traction rods running clear through his arm, a Mexican blanket in his lap. Later I heard that his brothers put him back in the hospital.

Now Donny Brown and I crossed the road and headed to the Great Chasm. We hiked beyond the trailhead, then scrambled up a rocky hillside. We ducked into a narrow corridor where it was perfectly dark. You couldn't see your hand if you held it up.

We chimneyed over a high bench, then the chasm narrowed and I had to turn sideways. I probed downward with my toe and found only air so I knew I was standing on a ledge.

"I remember this place," I said. "I thought I was going to die here."

"Me too," said Donny Brown. "Young Tom told me that if I didn't suck in my belly and flatten my back against the wall I'd fall to the center of the earth."

Then Donny Brown flipped on his flashlight and I squinted. We looked down over the ledge.

We could see the bottom only three feet below.

He cut the light and we sidestepped along without talking. Finally we climbed over a car-size chockstone and the chasm opened up and we hurried down into the starlight.

When we got back to camp we made a fire. We'd run out of beer and didn't know what to do. The wine was too sweet and the fire was too smoky. Donny Brown took out the pills again. This time he gave me a sleeping pill and a painkiller. Pretty soon I felt great.

We decided that in the morning we'd go look for Gram Parsons' memorial marker. He was a country-rock singer who used to camp in the Monument. He said he was looking for flying saucers. Then in 1974 he rode his motorcycle to the Joshua Tree Inn and shot dope with a woman who was not his wife and died a few hours later.

His remains were to be shipped to his stepfather in New Orleans, but he had told his friends that he wanted his body to stay in the desert. His manager drove a borrowed hearse onto the tarmac at LAX and, with some forged documents, lifted the corpse and drove it back to Joshua Tree. At Indian Cove he dumped the coffin roadside, soaked it with kerosene, and lit it. The fire went out before the body was fully cremated. One thing I like about Gram Parsons is that nothing he did ever worked out right.

When we woke up the next afternoon the weather was not very warm and there was nothing to do. We covered some sleeping pills with peanut butter and offered them to the little chipmunks. They weren't hungry. I guess we decided not to go see the Gram Parsons marker rock. Later a big van pulled in to the next site over. Five boys who were probably in junior high school got out and lit cigarettes. The smallest of them walked to where we were sitting at the picnic table.

"You smoke herb?" he said.

We smoked with this kid. His friends came over but none of them said much. We smoked some more. It didn't do anything. Trevor, who was the little one, told us his mom let them take the van because Todd had his license.

We looked at Todd. He had acne.

"What are you doing here?" Trevor asked us.

"Just sitting here," I said.

"Are you alone?" he said. "I mean just you two?"

Donny and I both nodded.

"Weird," he said.

"We're cousins," I said.

Donny Brown asked if they knew about the Iron Door.

"What's that?"

"Let's go."

I knew about the Iron Door, but I didn't know where it was. We all followed in a line behind Donny out toward the Patagonia Pile then we looped behind the campground. Some of the boys lagged like they weren't going to follow, but Trevor shouted come on and they did.

"It's around here somewhere," Donny said. "It's on this side of one of the rocks. Just look for an iron door."

Trevor and me and Donny started walking around looking. The others stood there. It was getting dark. Then we found it, a sunken cave with an iron door bolted across the opening. Donny pushed the door and we all went in. Trevor held up his lighter.

"Weird."

Donny Brown told how when the Barkers ranched out here they had a son who raped a girl. The family didn't want him to go to jail so they hid him from the law. They locked him here in this cave and gave him his meals through this slot in the door. Donny showed how the iron slot still functioned. It clanked.

"There's bad men out here," said Donny Brown.

The kids smoked some more pot.

Now it was dark and Donny wanted to show them the Hobbit Hole. Todd said they should get back, but Trevor said, "What's the Hobbit Hole?"

"Let's go," said Donny Brown.

We followed Donny to a boulder as big as a building with a

natural tunnel running underneath it. Donny Brown and I lay down in the dirt and wormed into the opening. I heard one of the boys outside say these guys are perverts and this whole thing sucks.

The tunnel opened up so that Donny and I could squat and lean against the rock wall. Trevor crawled in, flicked the lighter, and sat Indian style.

"This is it," said Donny. "The Right Now."

"It's a trip," Trevor said. He lit a cigarette.

There were names written on the stone with charcoal. The lighter went out and the red ash glowed.

"It's pretty cool in here," Trevor called outside. "Hey, you guys."

But no one else wanted to crawl in there with us.

Donny Brown stayed up all night fanning the fire and shooting whiskey and popping pills and writing a letter to his wife explaining that he was no longer of her world, that he was an outlaw by blood and that he might not be home for a while.

"Everything is different now," said Donny Brown. He explained that we didn't belong to the masses anymore, the people who worked for money and paid taxes and read the newspaper and filled up the movie theaters. He was really talking.

"We're outlaws," he said. "We're bad men."

When we left in the morning Donny's eyes were red and his face was pale. I didn't know how long we could go driving around like this. I had to get back home pretty soon and finish the painting job Shapiro and I had started. We drove south past the cholla forest and toward the Salton Sea. That's where Donny Brown wanted to go.

"Look at everybody buying and selling and lying and fucking and talking and talking and telling themselves that nothing is wrong." He popped his knuckles and stomped his feet. You only get a certain amount of space in this life, he said, and most people just fill it up with fancy junk and clever ideas and what a bunch of shit that is. Well Donny Brown didn't want his space full. He wanted it empty. He pointed at the desert as it sped by.

"Look how empty it is," he said. "It's free."

We stopped in Mecca to mail Donny's letter. There were plywood shacks with graffiti in the rows of palm trees and the air smelled like fresh manure. Metal silos shone in the sun. We drove south.

For centuries the Salton Sink had been a hot dry hole in the ground whose bottom was 250 feet below sea level. When developers dug a canal from the Colorado River they turned the sink into a garden and renamed it the Imperial Valley. But then the Colorado flooded its banks, busted through the dams and levees and rushed into the Valley. President Teddy Roosevelt ordered a team of engineers to turn the river back, and for two years they worked day and night with locomotive, dredge, barge, steam shovel, mule team plow and Indian labor crews. By the time they succeeded, the brand-new Salton Sea covered 600 square miles and was 79 feet deep.

Then waterskiing was invented and the Salton Sea became a resort. There were boat marinas and hot dog stands and pretty sand beaches. But when the water turned salty and the lake level rose, the beachfronts were flooded, and things went out of business. Better waterskiing lakes were built on the Colorado River.

As we drove into Salton Beach it didn't seem like a vacation place. A hot, foul, wharfy wind blew. The Salton Sea smelled like dead fish.

The streets were wide and empty and most of the houses were boarded up. A few had open windows and green grass and one had a dune buggy for sale parked on the lawn. We saw a man washing his car on the lawn with a garden hose. The neighbor's front door said Eat Pussy in spray paint.

I parked the car at the edge of the lake in Salton Beach and we got out. It looked like the world had ended. A crust of salt stuck to everything and water lines were bleached on the sides of buildings two feet off the ground. Deformed palm trees bent toward the earth. On the shore, oily lake water lapped over the corpses of a thousand dead fish.

"Carp, probably," said Donny Brown.

We looked around the abandoned buildings. The filling station had stacks of receipts and unused belts and a big Ford truck with flat tires and the windows smashed. Through the broken window of a motel I saw a drinking glass wrapped in sanitary plastic, a dusty pair of waterskis, and a portrait of Satan in red spray paint. A gull rushed past me and out the window.

"I'm staying here," said Donny Brown. "You oughta stay too."

"I have to go to work," I said. "I have to paint a condo. What do you mean, stay here?"

"No one wants these houses. I'll find an empty one and move right in. This will be my base."

"What will you do?"

"Live a little," he said. "We're not born on this planet to fill out forms and watch TV. Maybe I'll catch some fish. Maybe I'll hitchhike down to Brawley and look around there. Shit I don't care. I can do whatever I want to. I'm an outlaw. I might even be a half breed."

"But what if we're not an Indian?" I said.

"It doesn't matter," he said. "I'm living in the Right Now."

His mind was made up. Donny Brown took his backpack out of the station wagon and set it down in the salt crust. He said that if I got around to changing my mind, I should come back out and find him. I said I would and got in the car and left him there.

CHAPTER 3

Navajo White

MANHATTAN BEACH, CALIFORNIA

I drove back toward Los Angeles through the sunny Banning corridor between San Jacinto and San Gorgonio peaks into the haze of Moreno Valley. I tried not to think about Donny Brown because he was in the past and I wanted to be in the Right Now. Instead I thought about the condominium in Manhattan Beach I had to paint the next day and how long it was going to take me without Shapiro. But I didn't want to think about tomorrow either so I concentrated on the billboards and tract houses and outlet malls that I drove past. The Right Now was sort of boring.

I was glad to finally exit the freeway at Inglewood Avenue and get through Lawndale to my house on Marine Avenue. A lot of people call it Hawthorne, but it's actually in east Manhattan Beach.

Marine Avenue is a four-lane street with a grassy divider and traffic and a speed limit of 45. Every fifth house has the same floor plan. It used to be called Compton Boulevard in all towns except Manhattan Beach, but then they changed it to Marine Avenue, so nobody would think their town was a gang area like Compton.

Because of the divider in Marine Avenue, I had to drive a block past my house then make a U-turn. I coasted down the hill, and as usual some guy was on my tail. I made a quick turn into the driveway so he wouldn't rear-end me.

My house was the one with the sign out front that said 2 Hour Parking Commercial Vehicles Over 3 Tons. I opened the garage and unloaded my camping gear, reloaded the station wagon with dropcloths and brushes and five-gallon buckets, then picked up the mail and went inside.

It had been a good place to grow up. My dad liked it because it was close to the freeway and not a bad drive to work. In the summers Aunt Rachel usually had a breakdown and Donny and Shapiro stayed with us while she was in the hospital. We rode our bikes to the beach and to the miniature golf and waterslides down by the 405.

The best thing was the Chevron oil fields across the street. We would drag our BMX bikes under the fence and race around the dirt roads shooting BBs at rabbits. Once we came across a coyote asleep under a bush and when it saw us it yelped and ran across the field. I liked the rolling dirt hills and shrubs and the way the oil pumps dipped down and popped up like rocking horses on the range.

When the oil was gone, the bulldozers cleared away the weeds and graded the fields for the new Manhattan Village. For months the sand blew over Marine Avenue and under the front door and settled in our cups and glasses. As we wiped the dust away my dad said that it would eventually improve the neighborhood to have homeowners across the street. But the first thing the villagers built was a ten-foot wall around their village and we weren't allowed to go over there anymore. My mom said at least they planted trees and ivy in front of the wall. At least it was nice to look at.

Now most of the houses in the neighborhood were remodeled and repainted and nobody parked their car on the front lawn anymore but instead hired a gardener to make the grass green and pretty. When my dad retired, he and my mom paid off the mortgage and flew to Guatemala to live among the natives. Now and then they sent a photo of themselves garbed up in tribal costumes or hiking down a volcano. They would be back in less than a month, and if I was still living here, I'd have to watch their slide show.

I wanted to move out. I had lived in this house almost all my life. After high school I got free tuition at the university where my dad taught and I scheduled it so I could drive to college after morning rush hour, learn, then come home at night when the freeways were fast. Once, I decided it would be more authentic to get my own apartment with modern art posters on the walls and cigarette butts in the empty beer bottles, but after a year of paying rent I decided I'd settle for inauthentic, and I moved back to Marine Avenue. Now instead of being just a housepainter living at home, I was a housepainter living at home who'd gone to college.

There was no modern art on my parents' walls. We had my high school senior portrait and a line of old photos and paintings of our ancestors. I went into the living room and cranked some rock music and drank a beer. I would have smoked a cigarette if I had had one. It felt pretty real. But after a while it was hard to really rock with my great-grandmother watching me, so I turned off the stereo and sat in the quiet and waited to get tired. I was stuck here.

In the morning I drove to work in my street clothes. Shapiro said it was good business sense. If some homeowner wanted us to give an estimate, we could bid higher when they saw that we looked and dressed just like them. It seemed like a good idea. But mostly I didn't like to drive around town in my whites because I was afraid I might run into someone from high school. They would be embarrassed for me when they saw that I had turned out to be just a housepainter, since everyone else was something important like a stockbroker or lawyer or movie producer or rock singer.

I drove down to 27th Street on the north end of Manhattan Beach. The streets by the ocean were wet from the dew and the sunlight on the water was mild. I parked my station wagon in the empty garage under the condo and went upstairs.

Rich people usually want their houses painted white. This job was the middle unit of a three-level condo, and the broker who owned it wanted it Navajo White. It was high-dollar property, a block up from the beach, and it had a better ocean view than the rest of the neighborhood because instead of houses, there was a big grassy park across the street.

That park has a story to it. Back in the 1910s there was a resort here called Bruce's Lodge, where people from L.A. came for the weekend. There was dancing upstairs and a cafe below. It was so popular that customers of the lodge bought some of the lots and built a small hotel and a few beach cottages. I always thought the beach must have been a bit more exciting back then.

The only problem with the Bruces and their friends was that they were black. A local realtor thought they might take over, so he lobbied the city council to make it illegal for Negroes to buy houses here. He didn't have anything against Negroes, he said. He just wanted to protect the property value of his town. When the council did not respond, the realtor realized that the two blocks of the black colony would be a good place for a city park. He circulated a petition, and in 1924 the City of Manhattan Beach condemned the properties, paid off the owners, and tore down the beach club and houses.

The condemned lots sat there vacant for thirty-five years. The city forgot that it needed a park. Later, when it found out it could get sued by the former owners, the city sent some workers over to plant grass and called the place a park.

I like the smell of latex paint first thing in the morning. Shapiro and I had already prepped the condo out before we went to Arizona, so all I had to do was change clothes and crack open a five-gallon bucket. The fumes smell good and they don't get you all wasted like the oil-base fumes do. I screwed the roller on the pole and laid the paint on the wall in broad vertical strokes. It went on smooth and quickly, covering up all the patches and seams and smudges and making everything clean and uniform.

By the afternoon the fog had lifted, and a man and woman set their lawn chairs on the sidewalk and sipped fruit juice from tall glasses. I kept rolling and soon my shoulders started to ache. I realized that all morning I had been in the Right Now, and that was why it had gone by so easily. Now I thought that it was a waste of the Right Now to spend it painting a condo and I started to think about Donny Brown and wonder where he was. The painting went slower. I kept looking out the window at the people sunbathing, then looking back to find roller lint in the paint and drips on the wall. Finally I packed up and went home.

It took six days to paint the walls and doors. On the seventh I was lying on my back in the kitchen sink working at a complicated bay window that protruded toward the park. It was going slowly and I was eavesdropping on the man and woman sunning on the lawn chairs. He was telling her that if they wanted, he could get a pair of Lakers tickets from the office.

"Or maybe when the tide drops I'll go bodysurfing."

"Look how clear it is today," said the woman. "You can see Catalina."

I looked out there and saw the island. I was bored. The movers had just left after delivering some furniture and boxes, and I had rifled through the pile and found a diary that belonged to one Kimberly Weston. The sun shone down hard and reflected off the ocean. I set down my paintbrush and picked up reading where I'd left off.

It would seem that the future tenant was thirty-seven years old, divorced, and earning $78,500 per year at a Santa Monica consulting firm. Up until recently Ms. Weston had been engaged to remarry. The reason for moving into this condo was to have more room for her and her fiancé. Then the fiancé skipped town and took a lot of her money and her stuff, including her Aunt Mary's pearls. Ms. Weston was afraid to relate this detail to her mother. I kept reading. It was nice out. A warm breeze blew through the bay window and I fell asleep.

"Are you the painter?" someone said.

There was a woman in a pantsuit standing in the doorway.

"I want to have a look around," she said. "I'm the one who's moving in."

"All right."

Ms. Weston stepped back and circled the living room with her face close to the wall. She wore perfume and she smelled nice and successful.

"Is this some sort of primer?" she said. "Why does it look like that?"

"That's how it's supposed to look."

"It looks dirty," she said. "It looks yellow and it looks dirty."

"It's Navajo White," I said. "That's what they asked for."

"This is what it's going to look like?"

"This is what it looks like."

"It looks dirty."

I stood in the kitchen doorway trying to block her out but she slipped past me to where the diary sat before the bay window.

"What's this doing out?" she said.

"What's what doing out?"

"This."

She was holding it.

"I don't know," I said. I picked up my brush and touched it to the windowsill. "What is it?"

"It's a book," she said. "Never mind."

Down below the neighbor walked dripping wet up the sidewalk. He took a beach towel from the woman who now balanced the juice glass on her belly.

"Did you see the dolphins swim by?" said the man.

"Weren't they pretty?" said the woman. "I counted nine of them."

"At least that I'd say."

Ms. Weston had started to open a cardboard box, then she quit and slid the diary into her purse. She turned to me.

"What do you think of the color?"

"It's fine," I said. "You'll like it when it dries."

She covered one eye with her hand and looked at the walls and then moved her hand to the other eye.

"I don't like it," she said. "I'm going to tell them I don't like the color."

"All right."

"When we looked at the place the walls were white. Not Indian white. They were white white. This is a different color. What do you call the color it used to be?"

"White white," I said.

"I liked it better when it was white white, when we came to look at it. It was white and airy and the sun came in the window. Didn't you think it was better before?"

She pulled a telephone from her purse, unfolded it, and dialed. The broker picked up and she started complaining and then went outside where I couldn't hear her.

I finished the window in another hour and was going around with a touch-up brush when the broker drove up. Ms. Weston had long since left. It was windy now and the broker came inside. He had a pager clipped to the pocket of his Hawaiian shirt.

"How goes it?" he asked.

"Just about done."

"I talked to Miss High-and-Mighty," he said. "Or I should say she talked to me. She said the color isn't white enough."

"It looks fine," I said. "Navajo White."

"Well anyway," said the broker. "If we don't keep the rich folks happy, then we get the poor folks trying to move in. And then where are we?"

"I don't know," I said.

"Mexico, my friend. That's where. El third fucking mundo. So I'll need you to do it over in the white white or whatever the bitch wants. How does that sound?"

"I'd prefer not to," I said.

"I'd prefer to bend Miss What's-Her-Cunt over the kitchen counter and poke her in the ass," he said. "But you and I aren't in this business for our preferences, are we now?"

"I guess not," I said. "Still I'd prefer not to."

This caused the broker to laugh and slap my back.

"That's why I like you," he said. "God knows I could go out to Lawndale and find someone to spray this place out for half what I pay you, but we gotta look out for each other, don't we?"

"I guess we do," I said.

"There's just two types of people in the world," said the real estate broker. "Do you know which they are?"

"I give up."

"Us," he said. "And them."

"That's a good one," I said.

Then his pager beeped.

"Must be the wife," he said. "We got Little League tonight. I'll bet Supreme Paint is still open, so if you go over and pick up ten gallons of the white white I'll cut you a check in the morning."

I followed him out to his car and he tooted the horn as he pulled away.

"You're a good man," he shouted. Then he stuck his hand out the window and rubbed his thumb and finger. "I'm gonna make this worth your while."

I dropped my brush in a bucket of water and got in my car.

But instead of going to the paint store, I drove home. Some guy was on my tail coming down Marine, and I slowed down extra slow to show him who lived here. He honked and gave me the finger as he downshifted and roared off.

There was no mail.

I went inside. Maybe the broker was right that it was either Us or Them. Maybe I had to take a side. It seemed to me that Us are the people who drive cars and talk on cell phones, look at the computer and wait for the pager to beep. Us does the least amount of work for the most amount of money. This makes Us very important. I had always wanted to be one of Us.

Them are the people who ride the bus and do all the work. They nurse the babies, mow the grass, pound the nails, wash the cars, cook the meals and bus the tables. For this they are very lazy. Us has all the money and when Them tries to take it, Us sends Them to jail.

Now I worried that I had a bit of Them in me.

It would explain a lot. When I saw Them lined up for work on the curb on Inglewood Avenue I knew I should hate Them for stealing from Us all the good jobs at the car wash and the fast-food chains, but I didn't. I knew They were taking over the ditchdigging and housepainting businesses too, but when it came down to it, I didn't care enough about my job to fight for it. And even if it was un-American to say so, I'd move to Mexico before I worked away my life at Jack in the Box.

I was no good at being Us. I went into the bathroom and yanked the string and the bulb flashed then died. That was all right. I could still see myself.

I looked in the mirror. I looked the same as always.

"Hi, I'm an Indian."

It sounded stupid and once I'd said it out loud I was glad nobody else was there to hear it.

I didn't look like an Indian. I didn't feel like an Indian or even know what one was supposed to feel like. I felt just as white as ever.

Well even if my grandfather was all white he had at least robbed someone and shot him in the leg.

"Hand over the money you son of a bitch," I said to the mirror. "Be quick and nobody gets hurt."

I wasn't good at being Them, either.

I decided to just be Myself from here on out. But after standing there for a minute I didn't know what to do differently now from what I'd always done before. I needed to get into the Right Now. I decided I would do the first thing that came into my mind.

I picked up the phone and dialed Donny Brown's house in San Francisco.

"Well get up here," said Annabelle Brown when I said who it was. "Donald's lost his mind."

"Where is he?"

"I'll tell you when you get here."

I changed out of my whites and packed all my clothes in a bag. I emptied the food from the refrigerator and pantry into a cardboard box and took everything out to the car. I opened up the hatch and switched out all the painting tools for camping gear. Then I locked the house and went out to the driveway.

When there was a break in traffic I backed onto Marine Avenue and drove off. I filled up with gas on Inglewood Avenue then inched up the on-ramp to the rush-hour traffic of the 405 freeway.

CHAPTER 4

Blowout

EUREKA, NEVADA

I have never been able to be Myself.

They say it's easy but I think it's the hardest thing. To be Yourself these days, you can never work for money and never say you care about money. If for some reason you get some money, you should spend it as fast as you can on drugs and cocktails and sushi to show everyone how unmaterialistic you are.

But if you don't have enough money to buy whatever you want, it's hard to prove that you are Yourself. And if you don't get money from your parents or a trust fund then you have to get a job, and then everyone can see you're not really Yourself but some conformist instead.

By the time I had driven up to the coast and found a campground with no one in the booth, I had figured out the problem.

I wanted to be Myself like everyone else, but all I could afford was to be somebody different.

The fact was I didn't really hate working. Sometimes I even liked it better than getting drunk. What's worse was that when I got money, everything for sale in the stores looked so stupid and useless that I couldn't buy any of it. Even the stuff that was unmaterialistic like cappuccino and rock concerts and snowboarding seemed a little overpriced to me, and the real spiritual items, like a trip to Nepal or a jeep or an internship at a museum, were way out of my budget, so I ended up holding on to my money like a total square. Even if I had the money to be Myself, I'd probably be afraid to spend it.

I lay down in my sleeping bag in the dirt. The batteries in my flashlight died so I lit a candle and watched it flicker. There was nothing else really to do. In the morning I drove on up to San Francisco.

Annabelle Brown was the only person I knew who spent enough money to really be Herself. She knew how to act. Annabelle liked me because I never argued and always let her buy me things, and when she talked about love and art and the meaning of life, I always made like I was listening and believing it. I liked Annabelle because she was good-looking.

We always got along well. I remember a hot summer in Chico, stuck to the sofa in my shorts when in came Annabelle Brown and lay right down with me. She was in college. She poured scotch over ice and we sat up and sweated till evening, when Donny Brown came home. He didn't even blink.

Later on we all three sprawled out on the king-size bed. I slept so hard I don't even know what they did all night. In the morning Annabelle got up in a long undershirt. It covered some of her thighs but not all. She put on a pot of coffee and lay between us under the sheet. She passed around a cigarette and we laughed and scratched and stretched. Then she started rubbing her foot against mine. I hadn't been in the same bed with a girl since forever. I rubbed back. It went on till the coffee was done.

Think how startled I was and how startled was Donny Brown when Annabelle threw back the sheet to get the pot and we saw both her feet tucked up to herself, nowhere near the action.

Annabelle Brown loved San Francisco. It was artistic and pretty and everybody there was so much Themself that they never had to get a job. As soon as Annabelle married Donny Brown she forced him to move there from Chico, even though he liked living in the country just fine. She said the city would be good for his career, and that he'd meet a lot of stimulating people, and besides, she thought it was very daring to be married to a rock singer and she wanted more people to take notice. Her father bought them a house on Fell Street, overlooking the Panhandle Park. It was the fancy kind of townhouse with high ceilings and frilly little multicolored wood carvings everywhere. Whenever I went to San Francisco I felt sorry for the housepainters.

Annabelle Brown was home when I rang the buzzer, and when she saw me through the peephole she threw open the door and squeaked and kissed me on both cheeks.

"I've been waiting all day for someone worthwhile to talk to," she shouted.

Annabelle blew the curls from her face and towed me to a faded velvet loveseat and poured out the liquor and lit cigarettes and squeezed my hand and laughed and talked and pretty soon I was on my second scotch. The room was warm and smoky with the orange sun burning in the window and an electric air cleaner whirring in the corner. An antique lamp was rusted like her eyes, and everything matched her just right. The well-worn rug on the hardwood floor was the same burnt red as her lips. Annabelle leaned close and whispered stories in a bouncing song that now and then dropped to a purr as her hand landed on my knee. When she tossed her head to giggle, her dark curls swung into the sunlight, hung there golden for a second, then collided against her shoulders.

I liked the show, but finally I couldn't hold off any longer.

"What did Donny say when he called here?"

Annabelle slumped into the seat and shrugged and drank whiskey. "He was in Bakersfield. On the way to Chico."

"Did you get his letter?"

"Chico is what he says when he doesn't want me to know he's going to Oroville to score drugs."

"He's living in the Right Now."

"He's always got a new way to say drug binge. Now he's an outlaw. What's he going to do, get a horse?"

I wasn't sure if I was supposed to answer that so I didn't. I'd seen Donny Brown eat plenty of pills, but I'd never heard him called a doper.

"He probably told you he was through with me. I'll bet he didn't mention that I left him last month, before he got the idea to run away."

She put a cigarette in my mouth and lit it.

"My sister got married in Colorado and I was just going to stay out there after the wedding. You know, for a change. To have a little break from Donald. It's pretty out there."

The room was so close to the street that when the cars zoomed by I could feel it in my feet. I scratched my initials in the upholstery then rubbed them out.

"Have you ever heard of Telluride?" said Annabelle Brown. "That's where I went for the stupid wedding. I totally wore a brown dress."

I kept drinking and nodding. This made it comfortable because I didn't have to wonder what to think or say. If she wanted me to care, I could care. Or if she wanted me to be sincere, I could be that.

"But after a few weeks I realized I didn't need to prove anything to Donald, so I came back. Besides, the stupid car wasn't working right."

"Broke down?"

"Almost. And then when I got home he said he was running off to find his mother."

Now the sun had set and Annabelle's hair hung limp in her face. She leaned against me. She smelled good.

"Just like that," she said. "Skedaddle."

I patted her shoulder but it didn't feel right so I topped off the tumblers instead. Annabelle could drink about twice as fast as me.

"This is a nice room," I said.

She lit a cigarette and smoked the whole thing.

"Let's not talk about Donald anymore," she said. "He's immature, that's all."

I crossed my legs and sunk deeper into the loveseat.

"It's not a weakness to want to be with someone," she said. "It doesn't mean I'm not independent."

I said sure.

"I'm independent enough to know that I don't have to be alone all the time."

"Will you mix me another one?" I said.

"Everyone thinks they want to be free," she said, waving a pair of tongs. "Ice? But they don't know what freedom is, and if they had it, they'd be terrified. They just want everyone else to think they're free."

"Thanks," I said, and snatched my tumbler from her hand.

"When people say they want to be free, what they really mean is they want to choose who it is they're enslaved to. Don't you see?"

I said it sounded all right and that I was pretty drunk now and thought we ought to go outside for some air right away.

"Anyway, I think it's healthy to be insecure about your lover," she said. "It makes you appreciate each other more."

Finally we got up and left. Annabelle wrapped a coat over her shoulders and put her arm in mine and we walked through the park and turned up Masonic Avenue. Some kids were beating drums on the sidewalk and a man was talking European into a pay phone. It was nice to be in the city with the buses click-clacking beneath the cables and all the pretty town houses leaning toward the street, and I felt bad when I had to bend down and vomit on the front steps of one. Nobody saw it and Annabelle tugged me along and we kept going.

We talked about other things while Annabelle smoked cigarettes. She showed me a photo of her nephew and I said he was cute. When we got home we climbed up onto the roof of her building where we could see the moon and the skyscrapers downtown. Trucks rolled up Fell Street and everything shook. A song floated up from somebody's window and we waltzed right there on the tarpaper and gravel. She was talking about going back out to Telluride. We went back inside and she spread a road map on the floor. Then I heard myself offer to drive her out there.

"That's as good a place as any," I said. "I have to go somewhere."

"You're a sweetheart," she said. I had never been called that before. I liked it. Then she kissed me on the neck. Her lips were warm and she left them there longer than I expected her to. While I was wondering what to do, she let go and said good night and went to her bedroom.

I woke up in the guest bedroom and while Annabelle drank coffee we decided that before we went to Colorado we should stop in Chico and ask around at the bars for Donny Brown. Maybe we could catch him. We drove down Oak Street and lined up in the traffic for the Bay Bridge.

"It smells terrible in here," said Annabelle Brown.

"It's just paint thinner," I said. "I kind of like it."

"It gives me a headache."

"You get used to it."

Once we were on the bridge the traffic thinned and we started moving. Through the bars of the lower deck I could see sailboats on the water. We got out of the East Bay and onto the 5. I didn't have to think of anything to talk about because Annabelle told me about the different kinds of art they had in the gallery where she worked and about the people who came in there to buy it. She knew a lot about the subject and she looked great talking about it. I told her that if I had a bunch of money to burn I'd buy a painting from her in a minute.

We got to Chico in three hours. I dropped Annabelle downtown so she could look for Donny. When I picked her up an hour later she said she'd seen some of Donny's loser friends, who said he'd left yesterday for the desert, maybe to Ciudad Juárez.

"Probably headed to los pharmacias," Annabelle said.

She directed me out of town into the peach orchards. We

followed hilly back roads through cornfields then took a two-lane highway into a pine forest. Climbing the winding road up the Sierras, the station wagon groaned and coughed, running smooth only when I brought it down to twenty miles per hour.

"Nice sound," said Annabelle. "That's what my car did."

I didn't know a lot about cars. A few years back I had bought the station wagon for five hundred dollars. It was tan. The wagon drove pretty well and I never had to get a wrench and make an adjustment. When we coasted off Donner Pass and into Nevada, the noises under the hood stopped. Annabelle didn't say much and then she slept. After Reno I dropped south onto Highway 50.

Near Eureka the Subaru began groaning again. Annabelle woke up and lit a cigarette, glared at the dashboard, blew smoke out her nose, then turned to the window.

Then there was a thump. I took my foot off the gas.

Thump.

The car shook and thumped again. Then ka-blam. The station wagon bucked and swerved into the other lane. Annabelle made a high-pitched noise. I steered to the shoulder and stopped.

Instead of an exploded engine, I found an exploded rear tire. I was relieved that it could be fixed. But I was also concerned because with a perfectly good spare tire I would be expected to fix it.

I did everything right with the jack and tire iron. Trucks blew past and I gripped the asphalt. It was hot on my palms. There was no shade anywhere. Annabelle corrected me when I started to put the tire on backward and shortly we were back on the highway.

"How long will it take us to get there if we go fifty?" I said. I wiped my hands on my pants. I could feel the blood in my temples.

"I thought we were going to crash," Annabelle said.

The engine revved up to a nervous whine then settled. The road was straight and straight and straight.

Then there was something on my forehead. It was cool and smooth and felt good. It was her hand. She rested it there like she was checking for a fever. After a bit she took it off and wrapped it around my hand. The sun was low, burning my eyes in the mirror. I was drowsy.

After a while, I pulled over and Annabelle drove. Once she got it into fourth she rested her palm on my knee and moved it slowly back and forth. I closed my eyes.

We sped across the Great Basin and the dry air rushed through the vents. I remember the humming of the motor and I remember leaning and shifting with the turns. I started to dream. I saw Annabelle sitting on a plank floor before a wide window overlooking a mountain or a cliff or something pretty like that. I was there with her. We toasted the sun rising over the peak with tumblers of scotch, and there in the early sunshine at Telluride we were very happy. First thing in the morning we were drinking scotch and were happy. The dream ended so I started over and watched it again and again with a new detail each time. Once I made it a fancy bottle of Irish whiskey and once I even heard the ice cubes knocking against the inside of the glass.

Then Annabelle made a noise like a dog when you kick it and I opened my eyes. We were not at daybreak in the Rockies but afternoon in the middle of the Nevada desert. The station wagon lurched as she downshifted and braked and pulled to the shoulder.

My cousin's wife looked guilty. She got out and walked to the front of the car then came back to the driver's seat. She closed the door.

"You need to do something," she said.

I rubbed my eyes.

"Go look."

Outside it was windy. The sun burned hot on the mountains, and clouds raced overhead. There was no cover or trees or anything, just a lot of flat brown dirt and dumb little dead grass. I looked at the front of the car and saw that she'd hit a bird. But she hadn't just killed it and let it glance off.

This bird was stuck.

Its head was lodged between the grill and the hood and the blue body bounced from side to side in the wind like a plaything. I cradled it in my palm. It was warm. It wouldn't come out.

I motioned to Annabelle to pull the hood lever, it went click, and the little corpse plopped on the gravel. With my boot I nudged it into the weeds and got back in the car.

CHAPTER 5

New Friends
at the Famous Springs

JEMEZ CANYON, NEW MEXICO

A lot of people from big cities are moving into spiritual towns like Sedona and Telluride where they can be Themself and get in touch with the Earth. A good spiritual town should have some Indians within 100 miles and good skiing or mountain biking within ten. The stores should sell turquoise bracelets and cappuccino, and there has to be a place to hook up a modem.

Annabelle Brown's sister had bought a vacation house in Telluride where she and her husband planned to live when they were not on vacation. Now they were on their honeymoon in the Caribbean, so we stayed at their new house with the dog and the cat. The dog had a normal-size body but was so low to the ground that at first I thought it didn't have limbs. Finally I rolled it over and saw there were legs, after all, it's just that they were short and only three of them.

The first thing we did after feeding the pets was walk around Telluride and go to all the stores. It was a clear spring day and the streets were wet from the snowmelt.

"I wanted to do what was the most the Right Now."

"Isn't it beautiful here?" said Annabelle Brown.

I could tell right away that it was a spiritual town. Some white people had dreadlocks. Though you didn't see any actual Indians, real paintings of them were for sale in the store windows. There were fancy gingerbread houses and candy shoppes and the air smelled like popcorn. Lots of people walked along the main street shopping and laughing. It reminded me of Disneyland, except that everything cost more and there were no minorities.

Annabelle bought a silver bracelet, a pair of sunglasses, a book about wildflowers, and a cowboy hat for me. She led me into an art gallery and I stood there while she told the owner about the gallery where she worked and about the painting she did when she could find the time. He had a suit. He had a ponytail. They got along well. He turned and asked if I was a painter too and I said yes.

"What sort of work do you do?" he said.

"Mostly interiors."

When the clouds gathered, Annabelle took me to a brewery and ordered us raspberry-flavored beer and some fudge.

"Isn't this good?" said Annabelle Brown. "It's so unique."

"I have a stomachache."

Then it started to rain. We went home and I got under the covers and lay there. Annabelle dressed and undressed and walked back and forth. Now that she had been to all the shops in Telluride she looked in the mirror and announced that everywhere in the world was just the same and boring and she wanted to go back home to San Francisco. Then she said she loved me a lot, but she loved Donny Brown more.

"Me too," I said.

I turned over and pressed against the wall and tried to sleep.

"Who knows?" Annabelle said. "Maybe tomorrow it will be sunny and we can drink wine."

When I woke up in the morning, I saw that the cat had murdered a small bird and dragged it into the bedroom. She was batting at the corpse with her paw, and downy feathers floated across the carpet.

Annabelle was still asleep and I went out to the front porch. The last of the snow was melting in the sun.

Now that I was in the West I saw that it was a big place. I didn't really have a strategy for finding Donny Brown. I tried to think what he would do in my situation, but that didn't work because first of all Donny Brown would never have reason to go looking for anybody besides himself, and second he wouldn't go sneaking around with his own wife.

But I wanted to do what Donny Brown would do. I wanted to do what was the most the Right Now. I wanted an adventure. Looking up from the porch I was trapped by mountains and trees. I wanted my space empty. I looked at a road map and saw that the closest desert was New Mexico. The Land of Enchantment, it said.

I decided to go camping.

By afternoon I had gathered my toothbrush and arranged to return in a few days to take Annabelle back to California. I followed U.S. 550 south, picked up a used tire in Durango, and soon the handpainted billboards in Cedar Hill welcomed me to New Mexico. Ice Cold Cider Ahead. Meat Processing Custom Slaughtering. It's Better to Be a Square Than to Run in the Wrong Circles.

I kept watching the road signs like they would tell me where to go. The green ones were useless with the names of towns I'd never heard of. If I knew where I wanted to go, I wouldn't need a road sign. The yellow ones had good drawings but gave no direction. Blue signs led me to a gas station in Aztec, but all the good stuff was on the brown ones. One brown sign told me that Aztec had won the 1965 All American Town Award, another directed me to a national monument. I was looking forward to a cool air-conditioned government museum with Indian pots and baskets and buttons to push that would trigger recorded stories, but when I got there the gate was locked and the park was closed, so I kept driving.

I followed New Mexico 44 to the Nageezi trading post where a brown road sign sent me south to Chaco Historical

Park. Soon I found myself careening claptrap down a washboard dirt road with the purple sun in front of me and a black wall of clouds behind. The thundershowers caught up and came thumping down on the dirt and riddled the dusty road with dark bullet holes. Each drop made a pleasing metallic plink against the roof of the Subaru.

By the time I entered the park it was dusk and a big moon glowed in the sky and the road wound steeply off the mesa. On the valley floor I stopped the car and looked around. The basin was surrounded by lumpy beige cliffs and dotted with shrubs and cacti. I didn't see any other people. So far I liked it here.

I drove on to where the road turned to asphalt. There were cars parked on the side of the road and people looking at the cliffs through their windshields and kids scrambling over boulders. I wanted to go back to my deserted basin but also wanted to see what was ahead. It was easier to press the gas than make a u-turn, so I kept going. Around the bend was the glare of electric streetlights where a fleet of cars and campers slept in a concrete campground. I found the host at his motorhome and asked if there wasn't someplace nearby where I could sleep for free and be alone. I was on an adventure.

"This county's parceled off like a checkerboard," he said. "Some's BLM, some's reservation, some's private."

His wife shouted something from the trailer that I didn't catch.

"Some local Indians been taking pot shots at trespassers," he warned. "Better be careful."

I didn't want to get shot so I paid the host five dollars and parked in a stall. It was a good-looking place, tucked in the crook of a low flat mesa. The rock walls sheltered the camp from the blowing dust but also captured the hum of the streetlights and the growl of the generators. It didn't seem very adventurous.

Once it got late and I thought I might be tired, I hefted my sleeping bag and a thick roll of egg-carton foam and marched up a loose slope to the top of the mesa. I lay down just far enough from the rim so that I couldn't see the settlement down the hill.

I was away from everything now and I thought Donny and Annabelle Brown would be pretty impressed. It was very quiet in the desert at night. I was in Indian Country. This was where people like me came to be spiritual. I lay there trying to drift into the stars but the moon was too bright and kept staring at me. Then I felt a spider crawling up my leg but when I unzipped my sleeping bag I couldn't find it. That happened a couple times and finally I dragged my bed to within sight of the electric campground below and settled down and fell asleep.

The Indians were the first people in the desert. They were very natural. In the old days before being discovered by the whites, they didn't know enough to call themselves Indians. They had never even heard of India. They did a lot of weaving and dancing and searching the Earth for food. It's funny that a race of people supposedly so in touch with the Earth spent all their time digging for roots and tubers and never thought to go skiing or whitewater rafting.

I thought I should try to appreciate them. In the morning I drove to the visitors' center and asked the man in the ranger outfit behind the desk what there was to do.

He asked if I had paid the entrance fee.

"What do you mean?"

He repeated it and looked right at me.

"How much is it?"

"Three dollars."

I shoved my hands in my pockets like I was looking for something. "I'll be right back. My wallet's in the glove box."

I walked to the car and drove away directly.

I followed the first road I came to and it led me to an archaeological ruin from some Indians. The ruins had been unearthed and partially restored and now you could sightsee them from a web of foot trails and informational signs. I knew that the broken stone walls were very spiritual because the Indians built them, and I walked around in a circle to try to get the best angle and have the deepest experience. But no matter where I stood, all I saw was a heap of broken stone walls. The signs explained that the people who lived there built houses, prayed to gods, and cooked food to eat it. Big deal, I thought. That didn't sound much more interesting than what people do today.

So instead of appreciating anything, I just lay in the dirt like an idiot and watched the sheep clouds float across the wide blue sky and the morning shadows inch up the sandstone. A cool breeze smelled like sage. I knew it was wrong, but I wished that those ruins had never been found and there was nothing out here to appreciate, because then there would be no pavement and people and fees, just another drive-fast dirt road through the middle of the empty desert.

On my way out of Telluride I had asked a few people where to go in New Mexico and they'd said Jemez Canyon. There was an Indian pueblo and a famous hot springs. I had nothing against taking a bath in nature and I thought I might like to see some real Indians, so I drove out of Chaco through Cuba to Jemez Pueblo at the mouth of the canyon.

I parked on the side of the highway and walked to the pueblo. The adobe buildings and dusty streets were a thousand years old. There were no power lines or stoplights or billboards. I read on a sign that Jemez was the only place in the world where people spoke a language called Towa. Other signs said No Tour Buses, No Soliciting, No Cameras. I stood at the entrance and watched a woman sweep her porch. She wore sandals, and her black hair was drawn back with a scarf. The laundry fluttered on a line. Even though she was in touch with the Earth it was boring to watch her. It made me thankful to come from such a bland culture that nobody came to my house to take pictures of me doing my chores. The lady with the broom kept sweeping and I felt like a jerk poking around her town, so I bought a taco on the side of the road and drove off.

Up Jemez Canyon the desert became mountain. It hailed then rained. The plain little village was replaced by fancy homes and gated retreats for Sisters of the Bleeding Heart and the Zen Transcendentalists. I guessed there was more than one way to be spiritual and as I spun my wheels pulling into a muddy parking lot, I hoped that maybe I could get spiritual too.

The rain would not stop, so I changed into shorts and started walking. I followed a steep slippery trail down into a wooded gorge where a big log lay across a creek. I spread my arms like a tightrope walker and gripped the log with my feet, then followed a trail of beer cans and undergarments up the hillside. Lukewarm water drizzled down the slope so I figured I was going the right way.

Further up were the pools. The sky had cleared and the sun was shining down onto some naked middle-aged people lying on the rocks. They were fat women and serious men all pretending to ignore one another. A silver-haired man was perched on a rock above the others like the king of the turtles. He looked me over with no expression at all.

I watched a woman knee-deep in the largest pool splashing water between her legs and under her armpits. A man walked into the woods and a moment later was followed by another. Steam floated off the water and it smelled like sulfur.

I stood there for a moment trying to look like I didn't belong, then noticed a younger couple reclining in a lower, smaller, more private pool. They were sitting there in swimsuits beside a waterfall that poured out of the upper pool. I climbed down some boulders and said hello and when they smiled, I pulled off my shirt and shoes and eased into the hot water with them. The man lit a joint and passed it to me.

These people seemed spiritual enough.

"We're from Albuquerque," he said. They were married. He was hairy and she was skinny. Both seemed a bit saggy and somehow off center. After a while the man got up and wiggled out of his shorts and stood beneath the waterfall. He rotated his shoulders and stretched and rubbed the water all over his plump body.

"He's got a nice item," the woman said to me. "Don't you think?"

"It's a fine one," I said.

It was a pretty impressive piece. I had never had a good look at an uncircumcised item, much less such a large one on such a little man. Actually I had never had much of a long look at any kind of item except my own, but that's not the same thing. When he was through touching himself and we were through watching him do it, he lifted a can of beer from the cooler and sat back down.

I noticed then that the two of them had a peculiar way of communicating. When the woman wanted a sip of beer, instead of asking for it she reached over and grabbed hold of his pecker just as easy as she was shaking his hand. Then he handed her the beer.

The woman undressed and ducked under the falls. The man squatted before her and doused her crotch with water. When that was done she sat back down and we all soaked for a while without saying anything.

"It feels real good to stand underneath the falls," said the man.

"You should try it," the woman told me. "It feels sexy."

"Are there any cold-water pools around here?" I said. "Where you can swim?"

"Cold water?" she asked. Her husband shook his head.

"You know," I said. "For swimming."

"We like this pool here," she said and pointed to the waterfall like maybe I'd forgotten which one she meant. "It feels good under the falls."

So I undid my shorts and laid them on the rock and stood beneath the warm shower. I stood there naked in front of the people. She shifted close to her man and caressed him and together they watched me. The water was warm and smelled eggy and I splashed it around my back and chest then bent backward and let it pour over my scalp.

"I wouldn't get it in your nose," the lady said. "I got a bacterial infection here in '87."

I pulled out of the stream and blew my nose all over the place. Then I sat back down on the pool. My friends let out deep breaths, leaned back, smiled. The woman reached for her husband's penis and he tipped the beer to her lips.

CHAPTER 6

A Fair Spot for
a Picnic

GREAT SAND DUNES, COLORADO

All this could have been Mexico.

I had driven to Santa Fe and was walking around some art galleries and gift shops. I wanted to buy something but the prices were high so I just stood there and read some history books. Turns out that when Americans were just declaring independence from England and hadn't yet set up La Migra, Mexicans had already been living illegally in our country for more than two hundred years. There were so many of them here that they had the nerve to call it Nuevo Mexico. The capital city was Santa Fe and they had villages with Mexican names all over Arizona and California. In the year of the American Revolution, instead of coming over to help us, the Mexican officials in Santa Fe were busy sending dos padres into the desert to find a short-cut to Monterey.

The priests were Fray Francisco Anastasio Dominguez and Fray Francisco Silvestre Velez de Escalante. Their quest was not just to get to California, but also to explore Colorado and Utah and Nevada, which they also considered their country, and to see if there were any Indians up there who needed their souls saved.

They set out for their adventure in July 1776 with a small party of men on horseback. All summer they rode through the desert, naming everything they saw after a saint, totally unaware that there was a war going on in Massachusetts. They discovered an Indian tribe called the Timpanogotzis living in the middle of Utah, renamed them the Lagunas, and vowed to return to Christianize them. When an early winter fell in October the padres abandoned their trek to California and back-tracked across the Colorado River to Santa Fe. Along the way they befriended some Indian guides, ran out of food and had to eat their horses, and carved steps in the sandstone to climb out of Glen Canyon.

But when Dominguez and Escalante returned home, the church didn't have enough money to build a mission for the Timpanogotzis. They never returned. The Indians were left unattended until 1847 when Brigham Young and the Mormons descended and renamed them the Lamanites and gave all the Utah towns good American names like Lehi, Nephi, and Mexican Hat.

A year later America bought Nuevo Mexico for a couple million dollars. After three and a half centuries of rule, the Mexicans didn't have much to show for themselves except some dusty old churches, and they must have been relieved when the Yankees showed up in Tucson and Santa Fe with their guns and gadgets and dollars and taught everyone to speak English and gave them a job.

As I walked around the Santa Fe shops, I couldn't tell Us from Them. The Mexicans spoke perfect English and the white people in the cafes trying to speak Spanish were actually from New York City. These days it's hard to tell who's what. If a Guatemalan lies around his village weaving and dancing, Americans will fly down there to watch him do it and praise him for being a spiritual Indian. But as soon as that Guatemalan comes to America and works fifty hours a week at Wienerschnitzel, he is just another lazy Mexican.

Santa Fe made my head hurt and stomach growl. I was hungry. I couldn't afford anything, so I went back to my car and drove north past Taos on U.S. 285. In the window of a roadside restaurant blinked the neon words Beef Burgers Buffalo Burgers Alligator Nuggets. I wanted a nugget bad but I knew I didn't have the money for it. Pretty soon I was hunched over a picnic table drilling a can of tamales with a flathead screwdriver and a blunt rock. There was no opener.

I was in the Rio Grande Gorge National Recreation Area. If you've been to Lake Mead or Lake Powell, then you know that National Recreation Area is just the government's way of saying, Come Here and Waterski, Be Sure to Toss All Rubbish into the Lake, Dunebuggies and Dirtbikes Welcome. They are barren places with free camping and pit toilets, and that's fine, because motor sportsmen don't care about trees and grass, they just want to get the hell away from people and cops and do their thing without a hassle. That's what I wanted too.

I'd pulled into Rio Grande Gorge because I figured I could squat for the night without some ranger charging me four or six dollars or worse yet, busting me with a fifty-dollar ticket for illegal camping. But when I looked around, there was no man-made lake with a houseboat marina and no RV hookups. Instead it was pretty.

Big green hills rose out of the canyon and caught the last bit of sunlight through the streaks of black clouds. Sage blew on the wind. This worried me because the prettier a place is, the more rangers there are to get you in trouble.

I was licking tamale sauce from my fingers when headlights swung into my site. Night had fallen. I tossed my kitchen items into the station wagon and sat behind the wheel wondering if I should deny that I planned to camp right next to the No Camping sign or if I should just flee.

"Do not go," called a polite, lively voice with an accent I couldn't recognize.

It was not a ranger. It was Bud Parruck, from Stratford, Connecticut.

Bud wanted to know if he could camp here and I showed him the No Camping sign. He frowned. He looked at it.

"I tink tiss is okay if we bote camp here," he said. He sounded like wind chimes. "I sleep in tee car."

Bud was small and dark and I thought he looked like Gandhi. But where I grew up, anyone with brown skin who wasn't Mexican looked like Gandhi. Or at least like the guy who played him in the movie.

We sat down at the picnic table. Bud smiled. He told me he had been born in Bombay and had since moved to Connecticut where he had a job writing computer programs. He was on a business trip to Albuquerque and instead of spending the last night in the hotel, he'd rented a four-by-four and driven up 285. He had to catch a plane home the next day.

I was miffed. I was in the middle of an important camping trip and doing pretty well at it, even successfully hiding out from the rangers. And now here was a computer programmer with a fancy car and a good job and a funny accent, the wrong kind of Indian, sitting at the same picnic table as me. I would have liked for him to please get out of my adventure, but I couldn't find anything wrong with him or any way to tell him to leave. I tried to think what Donny Brown would do.

"Let's go down to the river," I said.

"Down tair?" said Bud Parruck.

We locked our cars and walked out on the rim of the canyon. It was dark out and cloudy. We stumbled down the steep gorge with rocks sliding down around our ankles.

"Are you sure?" said Bud Parruck. I could hear him breathing.

Finally we emerged from the mesquite onto a beach with the Rio Grande rippling by. We sat down on the sand. The ceiling of clouds had split down the middle and now the sky burst into a million stars. Slivers of moonlight bobbed on the river.

"Tiss is good," said Bud Parruck.

It got cold after a while and we scrambled back up the crumbling talus to the mesa where Bud's flashlight died.

"Sheet," he said. "Now what we do?"

I pretended I knew which way the cars were and he followed me through the pinyons with his arms out in front in case he ran into something. We kept walking and still didn't see the cars. I thought I might be leading us the wrong way but didn't want to say anything to make Bud Parruck nervous. "I tink it's tee utter way," he finally said.

We turned around and after half a mile found the cars and got in them and went to sleep.

In the morning I woke up to the clean revving of Bud's rented sports truck. He saw me sit up and hurried over.

"I left you some bread," he said. "Now tat you're awake, I give you almond butter and toilet paper."

We shook hands and Bud drove off. I got up and found a note and a half loaf of bread on the windshield. I couldn't see why he left some stuff on the car and gave me the rest in person. Maybe in his upbringing it was rude or disrespectful to give somebody toilet paper without his knowing, when he's asleep. But I wouldn't have been offended. I didn't even use toilet paper.

ri Mark,

Good morning. It's past 7 AM and I better leave if I were to make it to Albuquerque by 11 AM.

It was fun running into you and going down to the river. I left behind some bread for you. If ever in New England look me up —

Bud Parruck
████████████
Stratford, CT 06497
(203) 381 ████

Today I was to meet Annabelle Brown at her sister's house in Telluride. We were going to discuss things and then we were going to drive back to California. I didn't know where to look for Donny Brown, but I knew that if I went back now I'd be housepainting in a week. It wasn't much of an adventure. I decided not to think about it and took Highway 150 to the Great Sand Dunes National Monument.

They wanted me to pay three dollars to drive in so I parked at the general store and walked to the road with my thumb out. Before I'd even reached the shoulder a van veered over and stopped. It was an old Ford with off-road tires and no windows in back. The driver jumped out and shook my hand.

"Get in!" He shoved a cold bottle of Budweiser into my hand. "Where you going?"

"The sand dunes," I said. It was the only place the road went.

The man wore only skimpy gym shorts, a handlebar mustache, and a tattoo of a skeleton on his chest. He slid open the side door and grappled with lawn chairs, coolers, a blowup mattress. A big black dog ran circles atop the pile of gear and a small blond dog panted in the lap of a hefty woman in the passenger seat. The man cleared a space around a bean bag and I climbed in.

"I love animals," he said. "Got a gila monster back at home."

His name was Stu, and when I told him mine he said it aloud a few times. Then he waved his hands and said some more names, but the only one I heard was Millie, and I thought it belonged to the black dog slobbering on me. Stu hopped behind the wheel, twisted the cap off a beer bottle and spun the tires as he let out the clutch.

"Three on the tree," he said. He looked back and grinned.

"Three on the tree," I said.

The two of them were from Canon City and were having an affair. The woman said they liked to get out of town because it was a small one and people gossiped and when they were together they didn't want to run into her ex–old man. The black dog bounded over my lap and humped my knee.

"Easy there, Millie," I said. "Be good."

"Just slap him," barked Stu. "The little fucker."

The woman talked on and on about her son by her ex–old man. He was about my age and no one could believe he made it through high school without getting his brains busted open or sent to jail, and now he was in the Marines at Twentynine Palms. She had a letter she could show me.

Later I learned that not the dog but the woman was named Millie. The dog's name turned out to be Nigger. The black one, I mean. The white one was called Whitey.

The sand dunes looked like a gigantic anthill spilling out tourists and hikers. They hurried in circles and crisscrossed the mounds in single-file lines. We carried our shoes across the cold creek and ambled up the dunes. Whitey had some sort of spinal problem that caused her legs to walk at different speeds, so now and then the hind ones overtook the front and she trotted off at a diagonal. Once we got to the soft sand, Whitey couldn't really move, so she and Millie stayed behind while Stu and Nigger and I pressed on.

"It's nice to get this sunshine," Stu said. "That rainstorm was a goddamn turdfloater."

Stu was a roofer and a trailblazer. He had to explain to me that a trailblazer went out into the boonies and cut trails in the forest. His arms and torso were muscled and leathery but his legs looked like they'd just come out of a cast. We trudged up the sand slope and Stu said his knees were bad. I was tired myself so we stopped one ridge short of the summit. We tipped our beer bottles for the last gulps.

"You gotta drink the butthole," Stu said and made a face. "No matter how bad it is, I always drink the butthole."

I put the empties in my backpack.

There on top of the hill the voices beneath us faded to a faint tinkle and I could hear my heart. The wind hummed clear and quiet like it was blowing inside of my head. Out beyond the dunes were wide squares of farmland and the Sangre de Cristo Mountains with snow on top.

"Damn these knees," said Stu. "I'm gonna run this hill."

So we stood up and hollered and sprinted down the dunes. Stu was fast and I ran hard to keep up and the dog yipped and nipped and got underfoot, and we leapt over a rise and somersaulted down the slope with the sand in my mouth, plopped to a stop at the bottom laughing on our backs with the dog's tongue in our faces. It was very fine.

After that there was nothing else to do at the Great Sand Dunes. The parking lot was crowded and the ranger was telling us to put Nigger and Whitey on a leash so we loaded into the Ford and left.

Stu and Millie had told me about a scenic and secluded lake where they had camped the night before, and now they invited me back there for lunch. I got in my station wagon and followed them along a dirt road through a gate directly onto a sandy beach.

The lake seemed to be an industrial reservoir. It was ringed with chain-link fence, and bulldozers and Caterpillars sat idle by the shore. Stu splashed into the water and shouted that it was fine, and I killed my motor and went in after him.

Before I was dry, Stu had stacked up firewood and lit it with gasoline and Millie was setting a picnic table with potato chips and beer and condiments. Stu set a tape player on the van and blasted Fleetwood Mac. Next came Elton John, then Steely Dan, and soon the Polish sausage was grilled. We ate and drank and smoked.

"Out of the trash, Whitey," Stu said and snapped his fingers.

Millie told me about growing up in California in the sixties. One time she took the bus up to Berkeley and sold hits of acid at the Three Dog Night concert. Black Sabbath opened up, and after that her ears were never quite right. Stu didn't say much about music, but twice he agreed that sure Led Zeppelin played a good rock show but it was nothing next to the .38 Special. Then he ran up the hill and peed on a bush.

We were there for a few hours. Now and then Stu grasped my hand and told me how glad he was to have met me. When we packed up, I told them I was headed to Telluride, but they said I should follow them to Canon City instead.

"You gotta see Stu's lizard," said Millie.

"It's not a lizard," he said. "It's a gila monster."

"Well it's not a gila monster, it's a hee-la monster."

I said I'd come. It was a sunny handsome drive winding along the Arkansas River Valley. We stopped once so that Millie could reach through the window and fill my palm with crosstopped tablets of trucker's speed.

"Take these," she yelled. "They'll make you zing!"

"Okay."

By the time we reached the Victorian in Salida, my heart was beating fast and my scalp tingled. It was the best saloon I had been in, decorated with carved wood and molded plaster just like Annabelle Brown's house in San Francisco. Stu got a couple cans of Budweiser and Millie got a cup of ice water and swallowed a handful of crosstops. Stu racked the pool table. Even with my hands trembling I was shooting pretty well. I won twice in a row but I could tell he was just letting me.

I asked how they had met and Millie laughed and said that fifteen years ago Stu had been bopping her sister.

We drove on to Canon City, which they said was famous for having more jails and prisons than anywhere in the country. Eleven, Millie told me. When we got to Stu's house, Millie fed the dogs while Stu ran to the market to get more beer and a pack of cigarettes.

"Used to smokem like crazy," he said and lit mine with a match. "But now I just like to watch other people do it."

One corner of the living room was painted black and dotted with neon constellations and rock band logos and psychedelic cartoons. Arrowheads and crystals were arranged along the windowsill. Stu put on a heavy metal record and cranked it. I sucked on the cigarette and my eyeballs pulsed.

The main attraction in Stu's house was an enormous dry aquarium with neon pebbles and a bright orange lightbulb where lived the gila monster.

"Yo Jerry!" said Stu to the lizard. "Come out and play."

But Jerry was nowhere to be seen.

"He's probably in the pirate ship," said Stu. "That's where he hangs out."

"Make me merry, let me see Jerry," said Millie, clapping her hands. "You have to say that or he won't come out."

"Okay," I said. "Make me merry, let me see Jerry."

"Come out you little bastard," said Stu.

Stu opened a little door at the base of the tank and reached in to get Jerry. He was careful not to knock over the plastic man in the scuba suit. Millie asked me if I needed a place to stay for the night.

I told her I had to go meet Annabelle Brown.

"Lucky her," said Millie.

"Actually she's married to my cousin."

"Nothing wrong with a little pump-kin," said Stu. He was on his knees with an entire arm shoved inside the tank. "Even if it's not Halloween yet."

He let out a big laugh and Millie told him to cool it.

"Fuck it then," Stu said. "Stay here with us."

Just then he reeled backward and tumbled onto the floor.

"Dirty fucker bit my hand!" he yelped.

Jerry the gila monster bolted out of the pirate ship and past the scuba diver and through the trapdoor. He looked at us for a minute, twitched, then leapt off the table and raced under the sofa.

"Cocksucker," said Stu, getting back on his feet. He charged at the sofa and with a big grunt lifted one end and stamped his foot. The muscles in his back rippled and veins popped out on his neck.

"Goddamn goddamn goddamn goddamn."

The telephone rang. It kept ringing.

Stu set down the sofa and kicked it hard then picked up the receiver. He pressed it against his ear and looked at the wall. Millie and I watched him stand there and listen to whoever it was. I looked under the couch. No sign of Jerry. After a long time Stu hung up and walked in circles, then stopped in front of the speakers and turned it up so loud that the crystals rattled against the windowpanes. He put on a headset and plugged it in. Now it was perfectly quiet. Millie and I sat on the couch watching him sway to and fro.

"That was his wife," she said. "She can be a bummer sometimes."

There was Stu, shirtless, bobbing his head.

"Today was so good for him," Millie said. "He never would have gone up those sand dunes without you. He never has anyone to do that stuff with."

I thanked her and got up to go. I walked over to Stu and put out my hand. He pulled the headphones down around his neck. He didn't say anything. He clasped my hand and held it there. His were strong and callused. Then he refastened the headset and I went out to the car and started to drive.

I should have taken their invitation and stayed. Instead when I knocked on the fancy oak door in Telluride that night with my hair on end from the last of the turbo tabs, I smelled like sweat and smoke and beer and I was nervous. I had come this far and all I wanted now was a hot sun and somewhere to go next.

The door swung open and I squinted into the indoor light at Annabelle Brown and her sister and her sister's husband, all smartly dressed and toting tall clear drinks.

"Here comes the mountain man," said the sister with a giggle. She was wearing moccasins.

"If it isn't Liver-Eatin Johnson," said the husband. "Did you kill us a ki-yote?"

There they were with their terrible grins in the shocking electric light of the gingerbread house. I could hear the ice clinking in the glasses.

"Well did you bag a ki-yote?" said the husband again.

"It's in the car," I said. "Let me go get it."

I retraced my steps to the station wagon and put the key in the ignition.

"Did you hear, honey?" came the man's voice. "Liver-Eatin Johnson's gone to get us the ki-yote."

I put it in neutral and the car rolled quietly down the hill, and when I let out the clutch, the motor coughed and chugged and I gassed it and headed back to the highway.

PART
TWO

CHAPTER 7

Young Tom's Good Advice

SALIDA, COLORADO

When I was seventeen Donny Brown and I took a rockclimbing trip to Colorado. Our friend Young Tom was a river guide for Wally Spolak's Raft and Kayak Expeditions in Nathrop, and he took us down the Arkansas. Afterward we sat around the guide shack and snorted snuff and chugged highrollers, a drink where you stirred a shot of vodka into a plastic mug of beer. Ever since then, I'd thought maybe someday I'd come back and run the rivers like Young Tom did.

When I left Annabelle in Telluride I knew for certain that I wasn't going to find Donny Brown. I gave up. But I still wanted to have an adventure for Myself. So I decided to buy one. But then I found out that with the six hundred dollars in my bank account, I could only get a four-day river trip. All the cheaper stuff was boring, and I couldn't think of anything to spend my money on.

So finally I said to hell with Myself and called up Wally Spolak and asked for a job. I was embarrassed that I couldn't afford my own adventure and had to work on somebody else's, but I felt better when I found out that the jobs Wally offered were so exciting that you had to pay him five hundred dollars just to get one. I said okay.

Once I bought his two-week guide training course, he would teach me something he called the Spolak Way and I could be a real river guide and live there in the bunkhouse and eat all the leftovers I wanted. It was a little like being Myself because I got to spend all my money on it, and even though I would have to work all the time, at least the pay was low, just $550 for a twenty-four-day month, which was almost nothing if you did the math. It still wasn't as Yourself as making rock videos or trekking in Tibet, but it beat selling out to the Man and painting condos.

Besides, I knew Wally Spolak wasn't some slick business-man in a suit who was going to rip me off. He dressed like a real cowboy. And on the telephone he talked like a real cowboy and I imagined that he remembered me well and thought I'd be perfect for the job.

"If a lad wants work," he said, "I'll give him work."

I told him I'd never steered a raft in my life.

"I can teach anyone to run a boat. Even you."

Wally Spolak ran the proceedings in cowboy boots and a hat and usually yelled even if he was standing right next to you. At all times a skinny Texan limped behind him saying Yes Sir and No Sir. The Texan announced to all us trainees that we were here not just to learn the Spolak Way, but also to demonstrate how much harder we could work than the person standing next to us. Each night at camp there would be chores needed doing and he would keep tabs on who did the most.

I was a terrible failure at the Spolak Way and even now I

don't like to talk about those two weeks. Not only could I not learn the Way, I couldn't even make the boat go in a straight line. The Texan cursed me, other guides sat me down and explained it to me, Wally Spolak hollered and whacked me on the head with a paddle, but still when I sat in the guide seat the raft went in a circle.

At night when we pulled into camp, I liked to climb trees and skip stones out on the river, and by the time I was ready to wash the boats and set up the toilet, someone else had already done it faster and better than me. When training was over and I still couldn't steer a raft, Wally Spolak sat me down in his office.

"If a lad can't learn this in two weeks," he said in his real cowboy voice, "he's not going to learn it."

I wanted to say what about the promise he'd made me and what about all the money I'd given him, but I knew complaining was against the Spolak Way. Instead I said I'd clean the warehouse, patch boats, pack the coolers, anything, just don't make me go back to California. I'd left there for good and now I only had a hundred dollars.

"It's my name that's on the side of the boat," he said, "and this company is only as good as my name."

It was settled. I stuffed my sleeping bag and carried all my things from my cot in the guide shack to the back of my station wagon. Wally gave me a phone number for Young Tom, who I hadn't seen since high school. He was living downvalley in Salida.

Young Tom answered the phone.

"Is Tom McKinley there?"

"This is him."

I told him who I was.

"Who?"

I said it again. "You remember me? Donny Brown's cousin."

"Oh yeah," he said. "Hey."

I couldn't think of what to say next.

"Where are you?" he said.

"Wally Spolak's."

"Shit," he said. "You better come down here."

I drove down along the Arkansas River and followed his directions to the Apple Grove motel. I wasn't sure if I'd recognize Young Tom. It had been a long time. Donny Brown saw him once in Texas in '88 or '89. Young Tom and Alfy the cobbler had rolled Tom's bus on the Interstate and just walked away and left it.

I recognized Tom right off. He was sitting on a picnic bench in the sun outside the motel with a can of beer and a tape measure and a power drill. He looked the same that he did when he was eighteen, small and wiry and freckled, except his lip was fat with tobacco and when he smiled I could see his brown teeth starting to rot. He hugged me.

"It's my fault you lost your money," he said.

"That guy sucks."

"I'd have told you Wally Spolak was the biggest, dumbest, most redneck prick in the valley if only you got a hold of me first."

Tom popped me a beer and asked if I wanted some lunch. I did. He led me through the motel office into a small living room off a kitchen where a woman with an upturned nose and a ribbon in her hair was pulling a pan of enchiladas from the stove. This was Sue, and she invited me to have lunch. While we were setting the table, her husband Greg pushed open the door in patched jeans and boots that scuffed the floor. Sue served the food and we all ate. Young Tom made sure that everyone got a few big spoonfuls of pinto beans from the crock pot.

"Keeps you savage," he said. "All the savages of the world are beaneaters."

Sue and Greg had guided for Wally Spolak for years, but he wouldn't pay them half of what everyone else on the river earned, so they quit and bought this motel and started their own river company. They were converting the warehouse next door into a boathouse, and this was where Young Tom and the power tools came in. He would be guiding boats when the season started, but for now he got free board and a bit of cash for building racks and shelves and benches, painting and wiring and drywalling.

Young Tom told Greg about me and Wally Spolak and he didn't do anything but take a long drink of iced tea and shake his head.

"Tom can put you to work in the boat shed," said Greg. "Till you figure out what to do."

Everyone seemed pretty pleased. The season hadn't started yet and the motel rooms were empty, so I could stay in one as long as I needed to. Young Tom extended his tape measure till it reached the door and held the case in his crotch.

"If my cock were eighty-eight inches long," he said, "I could shut the door with it."

I asked to wash the dishes, but Sue said she was particular about her pots and pans and would do it herself, so Tom and I crossed the dirt lot to the boathouse where the tools were. Inside, Tom was building a waiting room. He'd bolted two-by-fours on the wall and was mounting benches onto them. As

soon as he was done building we'd have to paint, and Tom said
he hated to paint. I told him I was a housepainter back in California and he said good, you got here just in time. He plugged
the drill into the extension cord and took a bit out of his pocket.
Then he handed me a ten-dollar bill.

"Your first job," he said. "Go across the street and get a
twelvepack and a can of Copenhagen."

We laid into the beer and the tools pretty good and by
nighttime the benches were built and primed. Young Tom
showed me how to work the drill with my pinky finger instead
of my pointer. That way if it slipped I wouldn't break my wrist
slamming it against the wall.

We talked about the old Joshua Tree gang. Neither of us
knew where anyone was. I told him that Donny Brown had
found out he was a bad man and disappeared into the desert.

"Figures," said Young Tom. "I always knew he was a savage."

He tried to show me how to guide a raft, drawing pictures
and saying words like ferry and eddy, and I nodded but didn't
really understand. I'd had enough of rivers in the last two
weeks. When he was done explaining, I changed the subject to
something else.

"It's not bad work," I said and pointed at our bench. "You've
got a pretty good setup here."

He said it wasn't bad and it was better than the concrete crew
in El Paso. He said concrete crew the way some people say prison
so I guessed it was one of those things you don't ask about.

Young Tom was married now. His wife was teaching school
in El Paso, finishing the term while he was getting settled in
Salida.

"My old lady will be up in a month," he said and looked at his watch. He seemed pretty proud to be calling her that. "She's got a job in the schools here for next year and hopefully I can find a house by then."

"Then what?" I said.

"She'll start squeezing out the pups," he said and spit on the floor. "And I'll start sitting on the porch in my johnsies and scratching my nuts."

The next day we worked and drank beer and ate a pot of beans and finished the benches by afternoon. Young Tom separated all the usable wood from the burnable wood, and we loaded the trash into the back of his pickup, covered it with a tarp, and drove out to the county landfill. The truck was a rusted and dented mustard-colored Ford that made a lot of noise and didn't go very fast.

"I love the dump," he shouted over the wind and the motor. "It's like *Sanford and Son*."

Crows circled over the landfill and we pushed the trash out of the truck and swept out the bed. Young Tom wandered out over the heaps of junk and came back with a monkey wrench and a couple boards.

"Nothing wrong with these," he said.

Young Tom had been talking about a condemned church that needed torn down. He had a plan to get the demolition contract by offering to do it for free. I hadn't understood what he meant, but as we left the dump he turned down a bumpy two-lane road and said he'd show it to me.

We stopped just before town. The wind was blowing and

the sky was purple. There in the high plains twilight surrounded by chain-link fence and barricaded with plywood boards was an old one-room country church. It was dignified.

We climbed the fence and hoisted ourselves through a high broken window and thumped down onto the floor. I coughed and brushed the cobwebs off my face. Dim light streamed in from above. It smelled like mildew.

Tom reached into a hole in the plaster wall and grabbed a fistful of electric cable.

"Copper," he said. "They rewired this whole place just a few years ago."

A pair of swallows dropped from the ceiling and squawked and rushed out the window. I followed him through the church and he pointed out what everything was made of and how valuable it was because they don't build with this quality stuff anymore.

"Sinks," he said. "A toilet. There's a full kitchen back here." Young Tom said there was enough here to build a brand-new house. Just look at the floors, they were fucking oak. And the framing was all rough-cut pine from 1895 or something, probably milled right here in the valley. Real two-by-fours. Two inches by four inches, none of this factory shit. He'd been in the crawl space too. The joists alone were worth five bills. I ran my hand along the smooth cold door jamb. It felt solid, and good.

"It's a gold mine," Tom said. "It's all I need."

There was no more work for me at the Apple Grove Motel so the next night after dinner I thanked Greg and Sue and packed my station wagon. They'd given me some tips about other river companies that might hire me, but after my time with Wally Spolak I didn't want to see another river. Tom had told me about a resort where he used to work up in Maybell and he said to mention his name and they might put me up. Nothing too exciting, shoveling horse shit, cleaning cabins, washing dishes and mending fences, but it would at least give me a place to stay for the summer.

He was sitting at the dinner table and he fished a business card out of his wallet and set it on the table. I was already standing by the door. He extended his tape measure at me.

"If my cock was 103 inches long, I'd hand you this card, but I guess you'll have to come over here and get it yourself."

Right out of Salida, I stopped for a hitchhiker who was riding his skateboard on the side of the road. He was nineteen years old and when he smiled, you could see silver crowns and flecks of yellow stuff between his teeth. He was trying to get home to Utah. In a cardboard box were car parts he'd picked from a junkyard in Pueblo. Everyone in this part of the world seemed to have a lot of junk.

"Smells like paint thinner in here," he said when he got in the car. We didn't talk much after that. Later that night we camped on the side of the road and in the morning I left him at Interstate 70 and cut north at Loma. But ten minutes up the road there were barricades. The road had been covered by a mudslide. I turned around and asked at the general store when the road would be open.

"We're hoping by August," the man said and scratched at a lottery ticket. He said the quickest detour to Maybell was seven hours back. I got in my car and pulled out the card Young Tom had given me. That's when I saw the list on the back in his handwriting. The lines were uneven but tidy like he had been writing in the car.

To do: *learn how to spell*
             Read
             learn about cars
             take walks outside
             write
             try to fish
             commune with nature

Don't—   *Worry*
             Stair at ceiling
             have make believe conversations
             stair in mirror

When I first read it I was embarrassed for Young Tom because it wasn't fair for me to know how bad he had it, but later on, when I'd seen what living does to a person and how it pushes you into the desert, I saw that what he wrote was the best advice I'd ever got.

I drove back to the Interstate and found the hitchhiker skateboarding on the on-ramp in the middle of the hot Colorado flats.

Where did he say he was going?

Moab, Utah.

I said okay, get in.

CHAPTER 8

Germs

The hitchhiker's name was Beach Philips. The car parts he was carrying were to fix up a school bus he had parked outside of Moab. He told me now wasn't the best time to be in Moab because of the Navajo sickness. Down on the reservation they were coughing up blood, convulsing, dying.

"It's coming down fast," he said. "I'm gonna have to clear out pretty soon."

Moab sat in a patch of green between two red cliffs. A vacant mill was rusting on the banks of the brown Colorado. It was hot and the whole valley smelled like flowers.

"Used to be the uranium capital of the world," Beach Philips said. He pointed up at the only house on the cliffside and said it was where Charlie Steen lived. Charlie made so much money on uranium that he had a private pilot fly him in circles above the town whenever he wanted to watch TV.

"There's no reception down here," said Beach. "That was back before cable."

Now the house was a restaurant called Mi Vida with a sign

" 'Radical,' said Beach Philips."

that said Tour Buses Welcome. We drove down Main Street, a wide bright strip of motels and gift shops. A thermometer on the street said 98 degrees and it was not even noon yet. Old men in overalls sat outside the Westerner Grill on plastic chairs with cigarettes and cups of coffee. One of them sat on a motorscooter and had an oxygen tube inserted in his neck.

Beach directed me to a place where I could camp for free. On the shady streets of houses, cotton from the cottonwoods collected in drifts in the curb. I drove out past a junk store, trailer park, and fruit orchard, up a dirt road to Mill Creek.

There were some tents and vans and school buses in a flat dirt clearing where the creek rushed down from a mesa. This was the home of the bus people.

"That one's mine," he said as I pulled up to a long beige bus with a dirtbike leaned against the bumper. "You can set up next to me if you want. I gotta go to work."

Beach opened a padlock on the door of the bus, set his box and backpack inside, and relocked it. Then he kickstarted the dirtbike and buzzed down the road.

I looked around. There were laundry lines strung between the vans and buses. Some guy had a car up on blocks and was fixing something underneath. Barefoot children were chasing a German shepherd. It seemed a fine place to start from scratch.

I'd been sleeping in the car now and then, but the wagon was ten inches too short to be comfortable in, so I found an open space in the shade of two cottonwoods and set up my tent. It was a narrow tube tent with a couple parts missing and I had to stake it to the ground with screwdrivers and straight sticks. I still didn't have any money but I decided it could wait. I'd think about it later. I pulled a low lawn chair into the shallow creek and as the water ran across my lap let the day pass me by.

That night Beach Philips buzzed up on his Enduro with a pizza box balanced on the handlebars and a backpack of beer he had lifted from the walk-in.

"If you're hungry, you can have this," he said. "It's got olives. We were just gonna chuck it."

The sun rested atop the rim on the other side of the Moab valley. Dust rose from beneath growling jeeps and floated upcanyon. The sweet flowery smell was all around. The beer tasted good and cold.

So I ate the pie.

Beach Philips told me his real job was driving heavy equipment, but during the tourist season construction was slow so he picked up a few shifts at Pasta Jack's.

"Cash money in hand," he said.

He also worked as a river guide sometimes but said any jackass could do that job, just a buttwiper for rich people.

"They can?" I said.

"And besides it doesn't pay squat."

The sun dropped behind the cliff and a shadow spread over the creek. We slapped at mosquitoes then built a fire to keep them away. Beach Philips looked over at my tube tent.

"What's that?" he said. "The dog's tent?"

"I don't have a dog."

"Ghetto."

"I live in there."

"Woof woof," he said. "I'll bet it doesn't even keep the bugs out."

"I'll bet it does."

"See how yaur," he said. "I told you about the plague and now you're living down in the dirt in a dog tent. It'll strike you down like those Indians."

I opened another beer.

"All diseases are the result of human filth," he said. "You know that, don't you?"

"Sure."

"Flies, mosquitoes, they weren't even on this planet in the caveman days. They're the result of human filth. Spawned right out of the trash heap."

Beach slid a shiny harmonica from his shirt pocket and blew into it. It squawked like a chicken. His cheeks ballooned and blood rushed to his eyeballs. It didn't look good. Finally Beach set the thing in the dirt.

"I love that smell," I said. "That flowery shit, whatever it is."

"Russian olive," Beach said. "It's the worst if you grow up around it. There was a thicket of it behind our house. I'd get torn up in there on the thorns."

The fire had burned down to the coals and there was no more wood.

"Wanna see my bus?" he said.

We climbed inside and Beach clicked on a floodlight. All the seats were gone and in back was a wooden platform with a bare mattress and a sleeping bag. A stained sofa was pushed against the wall. There was sawdust in the carpet and some boards where Beach was building something. He said that once he saved up some money he was gonna trick the thing out with solar and water, and clear out for a while. I wondered how much further out there was to get to, but I didn't say anything.

"I'm gonna lay low with the coyotes," he said. "And once I get my stereo installed I'll be able to crank it up."

Beach Philips went to bed and I crawled in the dog tent. As I lay inside, the bug screen sagged and tickled my nose. The cicadas were singing. I lay naked on my sleeping bag while mosquitoes whined above.

It rained.

When it cooled off, the bugs left and I fell asleep.

In the morning I heard the clanging of rock against metal. I couldn't see anything from inside the dog tent so I squirmed out and stood and found Beach Philips pitching a tent that was dark green, domed, and handsome. He pounded the stakes with a head-size rock.

"When the shit goes down we may all have to live in tents," Beach said. "You'll want a good one."

I ducked into the dome tent. It was big enough inside that I could stand up straight. We stood around the big green tent and watched it for a while.

"It's a hell of a tent," said Beach.

I moved into the large dome. Beach was right. It was a fine home, waterproof and sturdy. There was room for a bedroll and my backpack and still some space I had nothing to put in. I couldn't think of anything else I needed. At night I pulled open the flaps and let the breeze blow through the screens.

I got a job cooking breakfast at a restaurant. I learned to flip an egg without a spatula. I tapped the panhandle and the yolk wiggled. Then I snapped my wrist and the egg hopped up and splatted upside down in the hot oil. I could flip three at a time.

After work I sat in my lawn chair in the creek or on the couch at the library where it was air-conditioned. I read about Charlie Steen, the uranium miner. He was a Texas oil geologist who was sure there was uranium in the cliffs around Moab. It was the beginning of the cold war and the government was giving off claims to anyone willing to stake one. Down at Big

Indian Wash in 1951 Charlie staked out a dozen rectangles, gave them Spanish names like Mi Corazón, Mi Alma, Te Quiero and Mi Vida. He paid the county registrar the fee of twelve dollars.

A year later Charlie got a grubstake from an investor, enough to move his wife, mother, and four sons into a tar-paper shack in the whistlestop town of Cisco an hour up the river from Moab. In debt to the grocer and hardware store and with just one drill bit to their name, Charlie and Mama Rose sunk the drill into Mi Vida. At 197 feet, the bit spun off the tip and was lost. It was hopeless. They didn't even have their own Geiger counter. Steen took his deepest samples to the service station where uranium digger Buddy Cowger rolled out in his wheelchair and took a reading. The needle jumped off the scale. Charlie Steen had hit pay dirt.

When the first load was hauled out of Mi Vida, Charlie and Mama Rose celebrated in Moab with hot dogs and a quart of whiskey. Overnight he was a world-famous millionaire. He built a cliffside mansion and threw all-night parties for movie stars and miners and politicians, jetting in mariachis from Mexico and big bands from Salt Lake City. He flew up to Salt Lake for a weekly rhumba lesson and once had a ton of uranium dumped on a newspaper writer's lawn for a prank. He got elected to the state senate on a platform to cut taxes and loosen the laws on smoking and drinking.

Meanwhile the population of Moab went from twelve hundred to seven thousand. Every room in Moab was full and locals were renting out their lawns for prospectors to pitch their tents. Trailerhouses were parked along dirt roads and in vacant lots. There wasn't enough electricity and sometimes the power died in the middle of a movie and everyone had to wait outside till the town generator was cranked up again. With Mi Vida churning and construction of a mill under way, Moab needed more houses. A tract of them called Steenville was plunked down in the slough.

Beach Philips grew up in Steenville. His granddad worked at Mi Vida, and then when uranium boomed a second time in the seventies, his dad quit high school and got a job at the Rio Algom mine for seventeen dollars an hour. By the time Beach's dad was eighteen he was married with Beach on the way and he owned a three-bedroom house in Steenville, a Jeep and a Buick, a Harley-Davidson, three dirtbikes and a river raft. The miners drank whiskey all night long, sniffed coke on the sunrise drive to Rio Algom, then dug uranium for twelve hours a day.

Beach said that when he was young there were no laws in Moab. All his friends went to the bar with their parents and hid under the pool table when a fight broke out, and then the adults would ride two kids on the back of each Harley over the La Sals through Gateway and down onto the Navajo reservation for a poker game.

By the time the mine and the mill busted, even Charlie Steen was broke. He'd quit the Senate, moved to Nevada, and lost his money investing in cattle, aircraft, and gourmet pickles. Finally the IRS came to Reno and seized his office, house, book and rock collections and even his pet monkey named Ringo. In Moab, houses were boarded up and abandoned as the miners moved on to find work.

Now Moab was a tourist town and had plenty of jobs again. The tourists needed bike mechanics, waiters, river guides and hotel maids. They needed tofu and espresso so they could ride their mountain bikes faster. So I got the job flipping eggs for six dollars an hour.

My fourth day at work was on the Friday before Memorial Day. Town was crowded. By six in the morning I had boiled down fruit and honey into syrup, and by 6:30 the meat gravy was thick. Grease popped off the grill onto my boots. The tickets lined up above me. Two over easy, oatmeal no raisins, short stack, huevos rancheros extra beans. The waitress came into the kitchen and pulled a ticket off the line.

"These people walked out," she said. "Sick of waiting." Then Beach Philips swung open the kitchen door.

"The plague is here," he said. "The quarantine is starting. We gotta andalay toot sweet."

I launched an egg and it splatted on the floor. Beach said that a busload of Navajo kids had been turned back at the California border yesterday, which was proof that Uncle Sam was trying to contain the disease in the Four Corners. Pretty soon they were turning this place into an incubation zone. The oatmeal was burning and stuck to the pot. I looked at Beach. He was serious. He sounded like a person who would sit next to you on the Greyhound.

"We need to get as far away from anything as we can."

"But I'm supposed to work till Tuesday," I said.

"My friends have a houseboat."

Even if his plan was dumb, it was better than flipping eggs. I hung up my apron and told the waitress I quit.

Beach and I drove south past Wilson Arch in my station wagon through the rocky fins of San Juan County. The car and the highway felt comfortable. I had just quit another job. I figured this was how it felt to be a bad man in the Right Now. I twisted the radio knob for a station, got static, then turned it off.

"How did you get a name like Beach?" I said.

"My dad."

"So it's your real name?"

"It's a family name."

He was quiet for seven miles.

"All my family back to the pioneers have been in jail. I'm related to Butch Cassidy." Beach said his dad was up in Draper State for smuggling drugs. His dad had been pulled over on I-70 because the lights on the trailer he was pulling were out. Turned out the Cessna twin engine he was towing was stolen.

"My dad eats worms and berries and talks to the animals," Beach said. Once his dad got out of prison, Beach and he were going up to the woods by Pocatello. "I think he's got some property up there."

I told the story about my grandfather holding up the gas station. Beach liked it. He said that most likely everybody had some bad blood in them, some just more than others.

When we saw the Welcome to Blanding sign, Beach reached back and worked the zippers on his rucksack. He put on a dust mask and clear rubber gloves and tossed a pair in my lap.

"Put these on," he said. "There's germs everywhere."

It seemed like a stupid thing to do but I didn't want to argue. I had signed up for whatever Beach Philips wanted. So I put on the gloves and mask.

Beach said he wouldn't be surprised if this disease wasn't something cooked up in a petri dish by the CIA to keep the Red Man down. That's how it had always been.

"The U.S. Cavalry used to hand out blankets full of small-pox," he said. "On purpose. Pretending it was a charity. Wiped out the race faster than a neutron bomb."

Beach had me pull over across from the Cedar Pony and we watched Indians get in and out of pickups. They were eating pizza and corn dogs.

"They don't look dead to me," I said.

"It happens so quick."

"I didn't tell you I might be one-eighth Indian," I said. "From my grandfather. I might be susceptible."

Beach looked me over from behind his mask like a surgeon.

"You're no Indian," he said. "I wouldn't worry."

It was seventy miles to Hall's Crossing. We drove. Beach Philips caught a fly by smashing it on the windshield. Then he tore it in half on the dashboard and poked at it with the rubber gloves.

"Why do flies even have all that hair?" he said. "It can't keep them warm."

Lake Powell was clear and blue, circled by a bathtub of sandstone cliffs. We drove aboard the ferryboat and floated toward Bullfrog. Ravens hovered on the wind and the motor hummed. Beach Philips popped open two cans of beer.

"Thanks for buying," he said.

At Hobie Cat Beach there were people and tents and camp-fires and autos as far as I could see. Music blared from the open doors of high-clearance trucks. ATVs zipped through the crowd and boys pissed into the lake. I saw one person vomit. None that I could see was worried about the Navajo illness.

We perched on short cliffs above the lake and drank beer and watched people jump in. Silver speedboats idled close to the shore while blondheaded passengers rubbed each other with sun oil. Jet Skis buzzed about. A girl tore open her bikini top in midair and the boys howled.

"Radical," said Beach Philips.

Beach and I jumped off the cliff then dried in the hot sand and watched the college girls floating on inner tubes.

"You see that one?" Beach said.

"Yeah."

"You looking between her legs?"

"Sure."

"I bet she's got some brown betty down there." Then he lowered his voice. As for Beach Philips, he was staying off the beaver. Anymore, who knew what you'd catch?

At sunset we joined a crowd around a huge lakeside bonfire. A flat-fronted houseboat was beached in the shallow water. Onboard, women climbed to the men's shoulders. They tossed bottles and cans into a heap on the sand. Disco thumped from a U-Haul truck where a DJ was spinning records.

As darkness fell, the mob swelled around the fire and the shouting rose to a roar. Beach tapped my shoulder and ran after two girls. I heard him holler which one is Manny's houseboat and one yelled back who are you and he followed them away.

I opened another beer. It seemed that the fire was getting closer to the lake. Men standing ankle deep in water could spit into the flame. The crowd shifted up the beach and away from the shoreline. I laid my head on my knees.

I must have slept. I felt a tap on my shoulder. It was Beach.

"We're in," he said.

It was cold. I saw that the fire and the crowd were gone.

Water lapped at my toes and a fleet of ash and cinder bobbed gently in the moonlight. The lake had risen and carried off the heap of bottles and cans and debris.

I jumped up and followed Beach, hopped over facedown bodies and trash piles, and climbed a ladder onto a boat.

In the cabin Beach Philips flicked a switch but no lights went on. He said there was a couch to sleep on. Nobody else was in there. I stepped out onto the deck and pissed. Beach Philips started the motor and I heard it hum and felt the houseboat move out onto the waters of Lake Powell. There was something squishy in my pocket. I pulled out the rubber gloves and flung them into the lake.

CHAPTER 9

Maid of the Canyon

GLEN CANYON
NATIONAL RECREATION AREA, UTAH

People have called Glen Canyon the heart of the American desert. It's downstream from the confluence of the Southwest's biggest veins, the Green and the Colorado. The Green River brings in snowmelt from the Wind River Range of Wyoming, then picks up the Yampa and the White flowing out of Colorado. The Colorado River drains the Rocky Mountain snowpack and absorbs the Gunnison and the Dolores before sinking into the desert. From there the Colorado drops through the waves of Cataract Canyon and into Glen Canyon, where it's joined by the Dirty Devil out of Utah, the San Juan from New Mexico, and the Kaibito seeping down from Arizona.

Maybe the first person to call Glen Canyon a heart was Major John Wesley Powell. He was a salty old codger who'd lost an arm in the Civil War. When the fighting was over he got bored, so he set out to fill in the last blank spots on the American map.

In May 1869 Major Powell launched on the Green River in Wyoming with nine men and four oak boats, the *Emma Dean, the Maid of the Canyon, Kitty Clyde's Sister,* and the *No Name,* which capsized and was dashed on the rocks in the first set of rapids. The major had to be strapped to a specially mounted chair because, with his one arm pointing at rocks and hazards, he had nothing to hold on with.

They floated the Green to the Colorado then portaged the rapids of Cataract Canyon. Glen Canyon gave them a spell of peace before dropping into the Grand Canyon. It was a shady wonderland of calm water, sandy beaches and crystal waterfalls, and hundreds of side canyons. Powell found the spot where Padres Dominguez and Escalante had crossed the Colorado. Camped in a riverside stone hollow, the explorers were lulled to sleep by what they called the sweet sounds of the rock, and in the morning named the place the Music Temple.

They pressed on. They survived the last leg of the adventure on flour and lard and in September emerged on the far end of the Grand Canyon. Three men had abandoned Powell and on their hike out of the canyon had been killed by Indians. The major was already planning his second trip.

One hundred years later, our country dammed Glen Canyon and filled it up with water. Everything down there was drowned. The benefit of the dam was that it gave us enough water to move to the desert and grow a lawn and enough electricity to run the air conditioner if the weather ever got hot. It also gave us a place to dock our Chris-Craft and race the Jet Skis. The government honored the one-armed major by naming its new reservoir Lake Powell.

I woke up on Lake Powell to the smell of hot dogs. There was a booth with padded benches around an oval table. On the floor beside me, someone else's socks and t-shirts spilled out of a canvas duffel bag. I took off my shoes and stood up.

I was in a long narrow room. At the far end, Beach Philips leaned over a sizzling miniature stove to get at a miniature refrigerator. Brown grocery sacks and beer bottles sat upright on the counter and above them hung an engraved and lacquered plaque:

Welcome aboard the Maid of the Canyon.
Bullfrog Marina, Utah

"They're friends of yours?" I asked as I stooped down to the refrigerator. I got a bottle of Coors. "The people whose boat this is?"

"It's a rental," he said. "Hot dog?"

Beach slid me a frank on a paper plate with a spoon and we sat at the booth. I sipped the beer. It was cold. I pointed at the fridge.

"Not bad," I said and cut into the hot dog.

I looked out the cabin windows. On one side a creek flowed out of a canyon into a delta overgrown with tamarisk and willow. On the other side was lake. Whoever called this place the heart of the desert hadn't looked at it in a long time. Lake Powell didn't beat, or pulse, or pump, or anything. It just sat there collecting driftwood and Styrofoam against the banks. The weather was hot and stupid.

"Too bad I didn't bring my toothbrush," I said.

"Who needs it?" said Beach. "We didn't bring any food either, and we're almost out of gas. But I think we got far enough. It's clean out here. Look out the window and tell me it's not clean."

I looked at the lake for a while and said it was clean. I didn't mention the Styrofoam.

After breakfast we filled a backpack with bottles of beer and a sack of ice cubes. Beach Philips said that with the hot dogs gone we would need to forage. We disembarked the *Maid of the Canyon,* waded across a marsh, and kicked through the reeds to where the canyon was tall and narrow. Ice water soaked my back.

We splashed up the creek and drank beer out of the bottles. After a mile or two, I was near drunk and finally we reached a waterfall pouring into a clear pool.

"Dead end," I said. "Now what?"

"Let's go swimming."

We pulled off our shirts and jumped in, hitting the soft dirt bottom with our heels and kicking up mud into the clear water. We climbed out and I did a cannonball and Beach did a back flip. Then I found a flat rock in the sunlight and lay there with my fingers locked under my head. The golden canyon walls on both sides were varnished with black streaks like the sides of a tiger. I could feel the creekwater drying up on my skin. There was a cool breeze up the canyon. I closed my eyes and lay there.

"Crawfish," said Beach Philips after a while. "Lots of them."

I sat up. Beach was calf-deep in the creek and he waved me over. He showed me where crawfish lurked along the bank hidden behind river stones. He said he used to catch them when he was a kid. Get enough to make dinner out of it.

"You gotta sneak up on them," he said. "Else they see you."

He lurched downward and pulled back a crawfish between finger and thumb. It wiggled and waved its claw. Beach reached for another, recoiled and hollered.

"Fucker bit me!"

I waded into the creek.

"It's easiest to just grabbum," Beach said. He was catching crawfish with both hands. "But if you're scared you can pinnum first."

I made a slow lunge and yelped when the crawdad nipped me.

"See how yaur," Beach said. "Listen to what I say and do what I do."

He showed me how to sneak up from behind and press down the pincer with a stick. Then I grabbed hold of the torso. The crawdad squirmed between my fingers and snapped its claw open and shut. It couldn't reach me.

"Hot pussy!" Beach sang out.

He emptied the ice bag and tied it to his belt. We snatched up two dozen crawdads and tossed them in the sack and waded downstream. I slipped on a patch of moss and splatted down in the creek and laughed as the empties shattered beneath me. Beach kicked up every stone back to the delta. The sack bulged with crawfish.

The *Maid of the Canyon* was where we'd left it and we went in to cook the crawfish. We stood over the sink cleaning the catch. First we pulled off the tails and chucked the heads and bodies out the window into the lake. They were still moving. When we peeled off the scales we had about fifty pieces of muscle the size of a marble.

Beach let the faucet run until the water steamed, then filled up a pot. He dumped in the meat and set it on the range.

"It'll take a while to boil."

We sat in the breakfast booth and didn't say anything. I rattled some silverware that lay on the table. It felt pretty clean. We were floating in a dinette on top of what was once the most remote place in the U.S. On the wall before me hung a poster of a penguin and a puppy dog.

This was as far from anything as we could get.

Beach Philips went to the stove and lifted the lid. He poured out the water and dumped the meat on a paper plate. The juices soaked through and the plate stuck to the table. Beach squeezed on some margarine and we ate. The crawfish didn't taste like anything and made a gritty noise on your teeth.

"We shoulda washed them," Beach said. Then he bent down to the fridge. "Maybe there's some ketchup."

It was nighttime when we parked the houseboat at Hobie Cat Beach. The party was going again and nobody paid us any mind. We were hungry. We disembarked and walked through the crowd to the station wagon where a can of tamales waited. We ate it. I asked if we should find a newspaper and see if there was any news on the quarantine, but Beach said we had to hurry because any minute a posse could be on our tail. He knew a good place we could hide out. We took a dirt road through the Waterpocket Fold and headed to the Serramonte.

We camped in a cow pasture near Torrey then in the morning snaked through the canyons and crossed the Serramonte. The road reminded me of a big skateboard park where you could ride up on the banks of the concrete domes.

Finally we got to the dirt Hole-in-the-Rock Road. It was wide, flat, and well maintained. Beach Philips said this was the place people went when they had to get away from everything. The first whites down here were some badass Mormons sent this way to settle a new town. They were made of stern stuff. When they reached Glen Canyon, there was no way down the cliffs so they laid some dynamite and blasted the sandstone.

"It musta been rad," said Beach Philips.

Then the pioneers lowered their wagons through the notch and crossed the Colorado. They eventually climbed over Comb Ridge and settled in Bluff.

"Now Mormons are soft," he said. "But back in the day they were hardcore."

Beach Philips said the Serramonte River was one of the hardest places to get to in the country. We would have to walk more than ten miles through steep gulches and washes where there was no road and the canyon was too narrow for planes or choppers. The Serramonte flows into Lake Powell, and Beach said its side canyons are the last remainders of Glen Canyon the way John Wesley Powell saw it.

We were rattling along the Hole-in-the-Rock Road at roughly sixty miles per hour when I hit a curve and the wagon skidded out of control. When a car fishtails there is a correct and an incorrect direction to turn the wheel. I think I did the wrong one because when I opened my eyes, Beach and I were hanging from our seatbelts and everything was upside down. It smelled like gas and I was eager to be out of the car.

Beach's door wouldn't open, but mine did, so we both crawled out of it. Gas was leaking and I thought there would be a fire soon. We popped the hatch and chucked everything into the dirt. Sleeping bags, a stove, a backpack, some books. There in that pile was everything I owned.

It was worth almost a thousand dollars.

"I've been in worse jams," said Beach Philips. "This isn't so bad."

We sat there for a while wondering what to do until two ranchers in a big truck pulled up. We hitched my old climbing rope to their trailer ball and pulled the Subaru right side up and onto the road.

"Remember," one of the ranchers told me. "Paint side up, rubber side down."

My car was littered with broken glass and powdered pancake mix and had its roof caved in, but it was not ruined. Beach Philips said it was no problem. With a swivel jack, milk crate, two-by-six, and a big square rock, we raised the roof almost back to its original height. I turned the key and the engine started. We packed up and kept going.

Beach said that the other badass who came down the Hole-in-the-Rock Road was Everett Ruess. He left Los Angeles during the Depression when he was sixteen and lit out to the desert on a donkey. At first he told people he was an artist, but Beach Philips said that was just an act.

"He was trying to get away from the Man," said Beach. Everett couldn't stand other people because all they cared about was making money and ripping people off to get it. So for four years he just walked around the desert with his burros and climbed the cliffs and stared at the sun. It sounded to me like maybe Everett was trying to get away from himself as much as the Man, but I didn't say anything.

Then one day Everett Ruess walked down into the Serramonte and never came back. Just like that, said Beach Philips. Hardcore. His camp and his burros were found, but there was never any sign of Everett. Some people say he was murdered or drowned and that now his bones are at the bottom of Lake Powell, but Beach told me that Everett Ruess probably married a

Hopi squaw and laid low in the canyons for the rest of his life, eating peyote and dancing the Antelope Dance.

"Either that or he turned into a hawk," said Beach. "That's what I'm gonna do."

The next four days Beach Philips and I were in the canyon. If there was a posse after us or any diseases to catch, we forgot all about them. We walked down Red Well until it met Rabbit Gulch and splashed through the creek that trickled from Fiftymile Mountain to the Serramonte River. It began as a shallow wash and by night we had sunk into a glen. In the morning we walked in the shade of cottonwoods. A porcupine was asleep in a treetop. I stepped in quicksand to my knee and almost lost my shoe.

We followed the stream as it curved and carved past Hurricane Wash through a corridor of sandstone taller than a building. There were waterfalls and wildflowers and five-toed animal tracks. In the horseshoe bends we echoed back and forth and back and forth. The rock was damp with moss and springwater, and the leaves were new and green.

Down in the canyons there was no horizon. To see the sky you had to tilt your head way back, or better yet lie on the ground and look up. From deep inside we climbed a sloped wall and reached the plateau. It was hot and dry and flat and bright. All around there was only stone. To the one side I saw the Henry Mountains and to the other the Fiftymile Bench. It took some time to adjust up there, like when you wake up in the middle of a dream. We sat in the desert for a while then climbed back down to where it was cool and wet.

CHAPTER 10

Butch Cassidy Days

MOAB, UTAH

At the gas station in Serramonte, Beach Philips read in a news-paper that the Navajo sickness was a virus spread by rats down on the reservation. It had been contained and nobody had to worry anymore. He was a little disappointed.

I had lashed down the hood with cord and replaced one tire with the spare, but another still leaked, and the windshield was so smashed on the driver's side that you couldn't see through it. I was worried that the Subaru might not make it all the way to Moab, but Beach said it was fine and we should go the other way so he could show me Butch Cassidy's house.

I stuck my head out the window and steered through town and into the pinyon flats of Utah 12. Later I had Beach steer from the passenger seat while I worked the pedals and the gear stick, but that just made us tired.

Once we got to U.S. 89 we switched places and Beach Philips discovered that by staring directly into two small squares of glass in the spiderweb of broken pieces, he could focus on the road. It was like holding sunglasses eighteen inches

from your nose and trying to see through them. It was fine until you got dizzy.

"Butch Cassidy stuck it to the Man," said Beach Philips. "Stuck it to him good."

He told me that Butch Cassidy was born Robert LeRoy Parker in 1866 just the other side of the mountains in Beaver. He said his own family descended from Butch's grandfather. I couldn't tell if I was supposed to believe him, but I didn't let on. He was proud to tell me about it.

Butch Cassidy's grandfather was a weaver in England who'd converted to Mormonism. Beach said that back then the Mormons did whatever Brigham Young told them to, so when Brigham called, Butch's grandfather sold all he owned and set sail to America to settle the new Zion. After converging with the rest of the Mormons in Iowa City, the Parkers walked 1,300 miles with wagon and cart to Nuevo Mexico, which they came to call the State of Deseret.

"They were just trying to get away from the Man," said Beach. It sounded to him like a pretty good deal. All you had to do was join some kooky religion, and you and your friends got a whole new country to yourselves. "I would have told them I believed in anything if they gave me a chunk of land in virgin Utah."

Butch's parents homesteaded a farm in the Circle Valley and moved with the six kids into a two-room log cabin. It was tough living, said Beach Philips. Then when they tried to claim more land, they had a dispute with a neighbor. The local bishop who was probably corrupt anyway solved the dispute by giving away the Parkers' land. Butch never forgave the Mormon church for cheating his family. He quit going. He smoked a pipe and spent Sundays running the horses instead of praying. Now he was a jackmormon.

By age fifteen Butch was running with a pack of older cowboys. After being accused of rustling cattle, he mounted his horse and rode away from Circle Valley for good. Up in Brown's Hole, Wyoming, he worked as a cowboy under the name of George Cassidy, which he'd borrowed from his father's ranch hand Mike Cassidy who taught him to rope and shoot. After a while it didn't make sense why he should do all the work when the owners got all the money, so he started poaching a beef here and there. In 1897 he was sent to the Wyoming State pen for cattle rustling.

Beach Philips said that the rich ranchers didn't think two years was enough punishment for George Cassidy. When he was released, they framed him up on some more charges and he had to leave Wyoming on the lam. Now he was mad. He changed his name to Butch to show what a badass he was, and for the next ten years no name stirred more fear in the hearts of rich men than Butch Cassidy.

We crested a hill and looked down into the Circle Valley.

We weren't in the desert anymore. Green fields of alfalfa were spread between low rolling mountains, and big white clouds exploded in the sky. Over in the grass on the side of the road a handpainted plywood sign sat in the ditch. There was a cowboy on it, and it said Whooooaaaa! Butch Cassidy Home Open.

We got out of the car. The log cabin was leaning over, about to topple. Plaster from the ceiling powdered the floor, windows were broken, and there was a hole in the roof where the chimney had been. Fast food wrappers blew across my feet.

"I guess there used to be all the original furniture," said Beach. "But fuckers broke in and stole it all. Don't you think it's still pretty cool anyway?"

I said I did. Outside, a padlocked donation box sat welded to a pole. I looked inside and saw some coins. There was nothing else to do there.

We drove past the Butch Cassidy Motel in Circleville and stopped for milkshakes at a gift shop. The lady inside told us that Butch's sister had kept the cabin up until she was in her nineties. But after the movie came out, she said, treasure hunters took it apart brick by brick. Now the owner of the land was hoping to build an RV park there so he could make some money to preserve the cabin. But the backhoe driver who was supposed to dig the water main left town with all the cash and didn't do the work, so the project was on hold again.

"Butch is buried out there in the valley somewhere," said the lady, waving her hand. "The family's not telling where."

We drove toward Moab over the mountains on Utah 24. Down at Hanksville the desert laid out forever in front of us, and Beach Philips told me that what I was seeing out there was the

Robber's Roost, Butch Cassidy's number one hideout. Butch's gang was called the Wild Bunch. The other gangsters were Elzy Lay, Flat Nose George Curry, Will Carver, the three Logan brothers and Harry Longabaugh who they called the Sundance Kid. A lot of them had worked cattle in this country so they knew the terrain better than anyone. No posse wanted to go in after them.

The Wild Bunch robbed mine payrolls and banks and federal reserve train cars but none of them ever got rich. The money had a way of just disappearing. Beach said that there's probably buried treasure out in the Roost and someday he was going digging for it. As for Butch Cassidy, in all his robbing he never killed a man and he never got caught, and all the homesteaders loved him and gave him fresh horses and told the posse the wrong way to go.

"They called him Utah's Robin Hood," said Beach.

Just as we came in sight of Green River, we heard a police car squawk and saw the flashing lights behind us.

"Code red," said Beach Philips as I pulled to the shoulder. "They'll never trace us to that boat, and we're not holding. Deny everything and don't forget your mirandas."

But the highway patrolman didn't care what we'd done. He just wanted to tell me that the broken windshield was unacceptable. I said it would cost too much to install a new one and he said just tape one on. Fine. I drove to a junkyard and the owner gave me a slightly damaged windshield for free, and I set it in place and wrapped it with duct tape.

"He never got a good look at my face," said Beach Philips as I pulled onto the highway. "Let's get ten-seventeen back to the bus and lay low a bit."

It was hard to say who lived with us at Mill Creek. The bus people came and went. Schroeder lived in a '49 Dodge bus the color and shape of a squash. It didn't run. Like Beach he got around town on a dirtbike. He had a holster mounted on the gas tank where he carried his pistol. He said it got him respect from the cops when they pulled him over. A German mechanic named Hans who used to work at the Mercedes factory had an '85 International with a Bluebird body. His generator and solar panels gave enough juice to run power tools all day long and he fixed people's cars and motorcycles right there in the dirt. The two sisters Debi and Emmy had driven from Milwaukee in a Dodge Dart and had jobs serving cocktails at the Rio. They lived in the car, one in the front seat and one in the back. Buck was a big redheaded hippy who said he was the town queer. He lived in a tent. He said one day he was going to hitchhike to Santa Cruz where everyone was barefoot.

Beach Philips learned about a river company where two of the guides had just quit. I went down there. The boss was a gray-haired man with scabs on his face. He wore orange see-through sunglasses and a red jumpsuit that said Marlboro on the pocket. He dropped his cigarette in the gravel and ground it in with his slip-on tennis shoe, then shook my hand.

"Let's go in the walk-in where it's cool," he said.

In the refrigerated room he took off his sunglasses. The skin around his eyes was soft and moist while everywhere else was bright pink and peeling.

"Two of our guys just quit," he said. "We're in a bind."

I told him I had taken a class on how to be a river guide.

2083

UTAH RIVER GUIDE I□ II□

Name **Mark Sundeen**

. Address ███████████████████

City **Manhatan Beach**

State **CA**   Zip **90266**

Ht. **6'0"** D.O.B. **10-14-70**

Issued **June 10, 1993**

Expires 5 years from issue date.

Signature

"We'll start you on the first of June," he said. "Six training trips, then you get your license and go."

On the days when my name was on the list I got up early and went down to the boatyard to blow up the boats and get the people in lifejackets. Even at eight in the morning the yard was hot and dusty with a fleet of jeeps revving their engines and big silver pontoon boats being hoisted onto trailers with a crane. If enough customers showed up, I got on the groaning old bus with them and bumped up along Highway 128 to the boat ramp at Hittle Bottom, the start of a fourteen-mile stretch of the Colorado River called the Daily.

At Hittle Bottom the trailers would wait their turn to back down the ramp as guides heaved the rafts into the water. While we did this, the customers stood there in their lifejackets and video-taped it. They were from Europe and didn't speak much English.

I would do a pantomime to explain how not to drown if they fell out of the boat, then we pushed off and they all sat there on the raft while I rowed. Sometimes when I was rowing the boat sideways down the rapid or accidentally bumping into the trees on the banks, the Europeans would wave their arms and holler at me in their gibberish, but luckily I didn't understand it.

If my passengers knew enough English to ask what a certain landmark was called or what kind of rock that cliff was, I just made something up and they all seemed to believe it. One of the words they understood was Butch Cassidy, so I would make up stories about how he used to live right here on this river. They liked that.

I told them how the Wild Bunch got in trouble. How when they started robbing the big money from Wells Fargo and Union Pacific, the stockholders wanted their money back and hired the Pinkerton Detective Agency to stop the Wild Bunch, to hunt them down and if neccessary kill them.

It worked. By the turn of the century most of the bandits were either in prison or shot dead by posses and bounty hunters. It didn't look good. So Butch Cassidy made a deal with the governor of Utah. He'd go straight and take a job as a train guard in exchange for immunity. But when the representatives from Union Pacific were late for the meeting, Butch thought he was being set up and he hightailed it up to Wyoming. Before the company men could contact him, he'd already pulled a job on a westbound Union Pacific. The next year, Butch and Sundance and a woman named Etta Place cleared out to New York City and booked tickets on a steamer for Buenos Aires and a shot at the straight life.

Etta Place was a schoolteacher who could shoot and ride as well as any man. Everyone knows that she was Sundance's girl, but one of my best stories was that Butch was in love with her too. There is a real legend that before Sundance joined the Wild

Bunch, the most beautiful girl in Utah spent a winter out at the Roost with Butch Cassidy. Some people say it was Etta Place. I didn't know if it was true or not, but it made a good story and I usually got a bigger tip when I told it.

All my tips were spent during Happy Hour at the Rio Bar and Restaurant on one-dollar pints and plates of half-price nachos or chicken fingers. It was my favorite place. It was dim and cool and a fan blew and music played and no one kicked me out if I ran out of money. At Happy Hour it was packed with river guides and cowboys and sometimes a lumberjack, and later the cooks pushed the tables up against the wall and a rock band played while the hippies and tourists danced barefoot till one.

Debi and Emmy skipped around in their smocks and flirted with the boys, but if you really wanted a drink, you had to talk to the big waitress named Jenny. She always knew to bring me Miller instead of Bud or Bud Light and whenever I tried to give her a dollar tip she brought me another beer instead. She said thanks honey, but she made more in a Happy Hour than I did in a day, and I looked like I needed the beer more than she needed the dollar.

For Beach Philips's twentieth birthday the bus people threw a party. We pulled the buses into a circle and Hans drove up to the mountains with a chainsaw and brought back a truckbed full of aspen and oak. Schroeder and Buck went to the supermarket and stole a chicken and tortillas and hot peppers and beer.

Some river guides came up to eat. A few kids from the trailer park brought up a sack of weed. A VW Bug full of high school girls showed up and we all sat around the fire and drank beer.

Even Mad Albert the drunk was there, lying in the dirt and sipping a plastic bottle of rum. It was a pretty good party.

The girls had graduated that week from Grand County High School. They were loud girls in tight t-shirts who bragged about the futons and clothing they'd gotten for graduation. Some of them were moving out of their parents' houses and renting a trailer together. The one girl who wasn't shouting sat next to me on a rock and said her name was September and all her friends were the biggest losers she'd ever seen.

"Is that your real name?" I said.

"Like I could have made it up. It's not my fault my mom's a hippie."

September asked if I wanted to take a walk. I looked around and didn't think anyone would miss us. We waded up the creek in the starlight, setting down each foot carefully. I tried to think of something to say to a girl who had just graduated from high school and hated her friends.

"It's dark out," I said.

"No shit, dude. It's nighttime."

September walked straight-legged like a boy with her fists on her hips and her elbows scraping against branches and brush. Her knees dangled from wide bony hips and banged together when she moved. She wanted to know where I was from and what I was doing in Moab. While I was telling her, she tripped on a rock and fell in the shallow water. When I pulled her up she slid her arms around me for a second. I pretended like I hadn't noticed and kept walking.

"You could live anywhere you want," she said. "You have a car. And you chose here?"

"It's pretty here."

"God, you're dumb."

We reached the swimming hole. No one was there. The moon was rising above the canyon wall and frogs were croaking over the sound of the stream. September ran her fingers through her hair. It was dark and straight and split down the middle. She had pockmarks on her forehead and eyes like an eskimo and thick lips she could flatten into a smile that made me think I'd just said something stupid.

"Well," she said with her smile. "I'm already wet."

September stepped out of her wet clothes and dove in the pool. I watched her swim somersaults and do a handstand underwater. She splashed me with her feet. Then she laughed and there was moonlight in her eyes.

"What are you looking at?" she said.

"Um, your teeth."

"Do you think they're small?"

"Not too small."

"I hate my teeth. This one needs to come out."

"At least they're straight."

"Well don't be a jerk. Take off your clothes."

So I undressed and dove in. When I came up she was standing naked up against the rock shelf and said come here. I went over there and stood next to her and she kissed me hard on the lips and clenched her jaw and scratched me with her nails. The moon was bright. I wasn't sure how old she was.

"Why are you kissing me?" she said.

"I'm not."

"Yes you are."

Then she kissed me again. She was pretty good at it. She could have been a grown-up.

"Do you like me?" she said.

"I think."

"No you don't," she said. "I'm sick of that."

"Sick of what?"

"Everyone," she said. She kissed and scratched me some more. It felt all right. I lifted her up onto the rock and stood there between her legs. She showed her teeth.

"I doubt it, dude."

We walked back on the trail and when we got to camp September's friends were waiting to leave. Mad Albert had tried to kiss all the girls and when they wouldn't let him, he tried to kiss the boys from down the street. Pretty soon after that everyone had left. Schroeder and Hans and Debi and Emmy had stumbled into their vehicles. Buck was asleep in his tent. Now Mad Albert was passed out in the dirt and Beach was sitting by the fire. September told me to come to Pasta Jack's some night and she'd get me some free food. She was a hostess there.

"Like a Twinkie," she said.

I didn't get it.

"You know, a Hostess Twinkie."

"Oh, right."

"I'm funny like that. You'll see."

She and her loser friends got in her Bug and drove off.

"Where did you take her?" said Beach Philips. We were the only people left at the birthday party. I sat across the fire from him.

"We went up there," I said, pointing. "Do you know that girl?"

"September Contreras," he said. "We used to live on the same block."

"How old is she?" I said.

"Younger than me," said Beach Philips. "Her mom's like a witch or something."

I poked the embers with a stick and flipped a log and the yellow flame came back to life.

"What do you mean a witch?"

He said that when he was growing up, September's mom was always burning incense and doing dances and praying to the Goddess. He said all those jackmormons are into that superstition shit.

"She didn't act like a Mormon," I said.

"What's that supposed to mean?"

"Nothing."

"What did you two do up there?"

"Went swimming."

"What else?"

"Talked."

"Me and September go way back," he said. "Just so you know."

We played with the fire some more. We burned up all the trash and tried to melt a beer bottle in the coals. Mad Albert woke up and patted the dust off his pants and walked down the road.

Beach said that September's Mormon half went way back to the pioneers but her other half was Navajo or Mexican or maybe a mix of both. Her dad lived in Albuquerque the last he'd heard. That girl's all mixed up, he said, but you wouldn't know it just from just meeting her. She looked white. She talked white. She acted as white as anybody else.

After the first couple days of work the Spolak Way must have set in because all of a sudden I could make the boat go straight.

The water was high and it was fun moving the big rafts down the rapids. The best part was that I got a big free lunch out of it. But I still hadn't got my first paycheck. On the days when I didn't work or didn't get a tip I just ate ramen noodles in my tent. Beach Philips told me I could go down to Health Services and get emergency food stamps. I didn't think I was poor enough to qualify, but all the bus people said it didn't matter.

I was scheduled to work but some people canceled so I had the day off. I went down to the Health Services office and they let me right in to see an advisor. She asked me questions and wrote down the answers on a clipboard.

"Occupation?"

"River guide."

"Income?"

"None," I said. "Not yet."

"I'll just check unemployed," she said. "Do you have a mailing address?"

"Not right now."

"Do you have a place to live?"

"I have a tent," I said. "It's a big one."

"I could fill out the rest of this," she said, but she could tell me right now that if I was homeless and unemployed I was eligible for the onetime emergency issue which I could pick up tomorrow. She handed me a thick folder with the application for full-time assistance. If I filled it out I could get monthly food stamps for up to a year, but in the meantime there'd be stamps for me to pick up in twenty-four hours.

I walked out to the parking lot. A parade marched down Main Street with cowboys on horseback and the high school band and little girls in leotards twirling batons. From an eighteen-

```
        OFFICE OF FAMILY SUPPORT              *        Utah - DHS - OFS
        267 NORTH MAIN                                 Form 228 C Rev 4-90
                                                          24  30  78
        MOAB           UT  84532
                                            NOTICE OF DECISION
                                            DEPARTMENT OF HUMAN SERVICES
                                                     CASE NUMBER: 00275668
                                                     MAILING DATE: 17JUN93


          MARK E. SUNDEEN                  E M-3
          ███ NORTH MAIN
          MOAB           UT  84532


                  ASSISTANCE APPROVED - S
      DEAR MARK E. SUNDEEN

      YOUR APPLICATION FOR FOOD STAMP ASSISTANCE, DATED JUNE    15, 1993,
      WAS APPROVED ON JUNE 16, 1993.  YOUR FIRST MONTH'S BENEFIT WILL BE
       $59.00.  YOUR BENEFIT AMOUNT MAY CHANGE EACH MONTH IF YOUR INCOME
      AND/OR HOUSEHOLD SIZE CHANGES.

      IF YOU HAVE ANY QUESTIONS ABOUT THIS NOTICE, PLEASE CALL US AT
      801 259 6127.  COLLECT CALLS WILL BE ACCEPTED.

                          FOOD STAMP BUDGET SUMMARY

      HOUSEHOLD SIZE    1          HOUSEHOLD TYPE    REGULAR

          HOUSEHOLD EARNED INCOME                    $150.00
          EARNED INCOME DEDUCTION                     $30.00
          OTHER INCOME                                 $0.00
          STANDARD DEDUCTION                         $120.00
          MEDICAL DEDUCTION FOR ELDERLY/DISABLED       $0.00
          DEPENDENT CARE DEDUCTION                     $0.00
          SHELTER COST DEDUCTION                       $0.00
          NET COUNTABLE INCOME (AMNI)                  $0.00
          BENEFIT AMOUNT                              $59.00
          RECOVERY AMOUNT                              $0.00
          FOOD STAMP AMOUNT       _ _ _              $59.00




      NOTICE #SSAA              KERRIE H                      3374

          IF YOU DISAGREE WITH THIS DECISION REFER TO HEARING RIGHTS ON THE BACK
```

wheeler filled with cows hung a long banner that said, Butch
Cassidy Days Rodeo This Week! Some actors dressed as cowboys were having a fake shootout in the street.

I watched the parade go by. I couldn't move my car until it
was over. I opened up the folder and looked at all the forms I
would have to fill out to get the monthly food stamps. It was a
lot. It would be a lot of work. As the last of the horses clip-

clopped down Main Street, I dropped the stack of application forms in the trash can.

That night I washed off in the creek and drove down to Pasta Jack's. I didn't tell Beach where I was going. I liked the girl September and I could use the free food. The restaurant was a white stucco box on the corner of Main and Center in the parking lot of the Best Western. Since it was Italian, it had a red tile roof. September was on the patio in high heels and a fancy gown that showed the scrapes and bruises on her knees. She gave me a menu and led me under a trellis to an outdoor table.

"I like your dress," I said.

"I stole it," she said. "It was four hundred dollars at Dillard's."

"What's that?"

"Some rich store in Albuquerque," she said. "My shift's over in ten minutes and I'll come sit with you."

It must have been a good restaurant because the menu said it had locations all over Colorado and Texas. The first page had a drawing of a real Italian cottage that had tiles on the roof sort of like the restaurant itself. My table was right next to the street with a red checkered tablecloth and a candle burning in a red bowl. Between the patio and the sidewalk was a plaster wall painted to look like tile. The people next to me were speaking German or some other foreign language. It was just like Europe.

The big rigs thundered down Main Street, jamming gears on the overnight haul to Arizona.

I couldn't decide what to get. The manicotti with meat sounded good, but so did Jack's Jumbo Shells. September finally came out with a big brown bag and sat down with me.

"Dude," she said through her teeth. "I can't believe I work here. This place is de la chingada."

"You speak Spanish?"

"A little."

"Say something."

"Chinga tu madre. How's that?"

"Pretty good."

She rubbed her toes against my knee. The Europeans were topping off their wine glasses.

"I can't tell what language those people are speaking," I said. "I wonder where they're from."

"Probably Germans," she said.

"Or maybe Swiss."

"Swiss isn't a language, you dumbshit." She looked over at the Europeans then back at me. "It's not, is it?"

"I don't think so."

Some guys in muscle tees drove by in a pickup truck and honked at September. I liked that. The waitress walked up.

"This is my mom," September said. "She works here too. She thinks you're too old for me."

September's mother said hi and I said hi back. She had lines around her eyes and straight gray hair with bangs. We shook hands. She pointed at the menu.

"Need a little more time?"

"She's just working here to pay for my sister's braces," September said. "We both think it sucks."

Her mom turned and said she'd be back in a bit. Then September reached into a shopping bag and handed me something wide and flat. It was a watercolor painting on a piece of tagboard. A person was rowing a boat in a canyon and he looked very blissful. It was supposed to be me.

"It's really nice," I said.

"You don't like it."

"I've never been in a painting before."

"You think it's totally ugly, dude."

"I don't have anywhere to hang it," I said.

"You don't have to keep it. I'll take it home."

"Now you're mad."

"I should take some painting lessons," she said.

"Where would I put it?"

"Lean over here and kiss me."

Her mom walked up with her pen and pad and put her hand on my shoulder.

"Did she give you the picture?"

"He thought it sucked and he didn't want it," said September. "I'll have the gelato."

September's mom took her hand off my shoulder. A police car raced down Center Street and whipped onto Main with lights flashing and sirens screaming. It was followed by the Sheriff's Search and Rescue jeep.

"I'll have the Jumbo Shells," I said.

The next morning I worked a half day. I told the French people on my boat all about Butch Cassidy and Etta Place and the Sundance Kid. I told how the three of them were living peacefully on a ranch in Patagonia for four years until on orders of the Pinkertons, the local police came to arrest them. They abandoned all they had and went back to robbing. About that time two banditos yanquis were killed in a shootout in Bolivia. Some claimed that the dead men were Butch and Sundance but I ended my story with Butch coming back to the States and living the straight life in Spokane, Washington. I said there was still a question about whether or not Sundance made it back alive, and as for Etta Place, she was never heard of again.

I thought it was a pretty good story. If I'd had some Germans or Dutch or Americans on the boat they'd have tipped me big for it. Or if I'd had some Italians they might have taken me to a fancy restaurant that night and filled me with wine. But wouldn't you know it I had French people, so the story was wasted. Of course they stiffed me. And because it was just a half day I didn't even get lunch. When I got back to the boatyard I picked up the food stamps and then drove up to September's house. I was pretty hungry by then.

"Beach came over," said September as we drove to City Market. "He said it's okay for me to go out with you as long as you're nice to me."

"Look at all my food stamps."

"I love Beach Philips," she said. "I just wish he wasn't such a dork."

"Fifty-nine dollars' worth."

"Someday I'll just fuck him so he can get over me. He's been waiting for it all his life."

City Market was a superfancy supermarket. September said that every loser in town was proud of it. It had a hot and cold deli and salad bar and pharmacy and bakery and video rental. She told me that when it opened a few years ago, there was a parade down Main Street with the mayor and the marching band and a herd of grinning fat men waving flags. It made her embarrassed as shit to be from such a dumbass town. Personally I liked City Market because it was air-conditioned and the bathroom was easy to find.

If you've ever been hungry in a supermarket with an emergency ration of food stamps, then you know what it means to be a free person in a good world. I pushed a cart up and down the aisles and looked at all the things you could get. I couldn't think about anything. The rows of food were like stained glass windows, and electric light the color of honey sifted down from heaven on a happy little tune. The people on the cereal boxes were jolly. There was a whole wall of cheese. I looked at the snack foods and the soda pop and the canned fruits and the spice rack and the pounds and pounds of flour and sugar. I slid open the ice cream door and let the cold smoke float out. I handled the fruits.

September fed me a strawberry, then proved she could put seventeen grapes in her mouth. I got a piece of fried chicken at the hot deli and ate it right there and licked my fingers. We ate handfuls of granola and gummi bears out of the bins. She asked me if I liked licorice and I said yes and she stuffed a box in her backpack.

"You're gonna get busted," I said.

"Not even, dude. Put this in your pocket."

"No way."

"Chicken," she said. "You're a total chicken."

"I have food stamps," I said. "I'll buy you whatever you want."

She said she wasn't hungry and went down a different aisle. I filled the cart with fifty dollars of food and gave over the food stamps and pushed it across the hot parking lot to the car. September was already there. I had cans of beans and tortillas and rice and vegetables and cereal and powdered milk and noodles and spaghetti sauce. September opened her backpack and pulled out fresh pesto sauce, candy bars, Pop Tarts, rice milk, and a small tub of ice cream.

"I got you a present," she said. She handed me a quart of Miller and kissed me on the cheek. I asked her if she didn't ever get caught and she said never, well almost never, that she was on probation in New Mexico but it was almost over. We stood there in the shade made by the raised hatchback. It was hot out.

"What should we do now?" I said.

"Well duh," she said. "It's the rodeo tonight."

The rodeo was out at the Spanish Valley Equestrian Center. While we were driving up there September told me she used to be a barrel rider in the Grand County Rodeo. Two years ago she'd even been Canyonlands Rodeo Queen which included not only Grand County but also Carbon, Emory, and San Juan. She didn't ride anymore, but she still liked to watch.

Lots of the people in the parking lot of the Equestrian Center were wearing white cowboy hats and tight Wranglers. September and I sat on the back bumper and drank the beer and ate the ice cream. I still had the cowboy hat that Annabelle Brown had bought for me. It was there in the back of the wagon with the groceries and I asked September if I should wear it.

"Put it on," she said.

I set the hat on my head and she looked at me.

"You look like a dork," she said. "A cute dork, but you should let me wear it."

She plucked it off my head and looked at the label.

"Stetson," she said. "Dude, you're rich."

She put the hat on. It came down all the way over her eyes and she had to cock back her head to see out from under it. She shook her head from side to side and the hat stayed in place.

We walked past a gift shack selling hats and t-shirts with her in the hat and me following behind. The arena was bright from the lights bolted to the rafters. The air conditioner was on. This rodeo was being held inside.

The announcer came on and announced all the sponsors and pretty soon guys were riding horses and throwing lassoes. The wait in between cowboys was a lot longer than when you watch it on TV. A fancy new pickup truck kept driving laps around the field.

"I forgot how boring this is without acid," September said. She told me that a hit and a half of acid had been her secret weapon for the barrel riding competitions. "That's how I beat the Mormons."

A cowboy wrestled a steer to the ground and jumped up grinning. Everybody clapped and flashbulbs popped.

"Let's get out of here," she said.

On the way through the parking lot, we stopped at the gift booth and tried on ball caps with the different rodeo events illustrated on the front. When we got back to the car September took off the Stetson and underneath was a cap she'd stolen that said Team Roping on it. It was still light out, and the mountains were pink in the last glow of sunshine. I got this for you, she said, and I said thanks. Dude, she said, I like you a lot. I'd steal anything for you.

CHAPTER 11

Reservation Reservation

FORT DEFIANCE, ARIZONA

Wake drive lift row row eat row row row lift drive drink sleep.
Wake drive lift row row eat row row row lift drive drink sleep.
Wake drive lift row row eat row row row lift drive drink sleep.
Wake drive lift row row eat row row row lift drive drink sleep.

Fireworks stands popped up on Main Street for the Fourth of July then closed and opened again for Pioneer Day. The old men at the Westerner Grill smoked cigarettes in the shade beneath a For Sale sign in the window. The last of the snowcaps melted off the mountains and Tukuhnikivatz was bare and the river was a trickle down the canyon and the wind blew upstream and there were no rapids. Sometimes the Europeans got bored sitting there on the flatwater while I threw myself against the oars, but whenever they said so I pretended not to understand.

Monsoon season blew in. In the afternoon black thunderheads peeled off the La Sals and dropped a few heavy drops in the dust. Beach Philips quit his pizza cook job because he could make more money fixing people's plumbing and selling them quarter ounces. He said he had a basement lined up where he was going to grow a harvest and did I want to go in with him on it, but I said I'm the wrong person because I get caught at whatever I do. The rangers staked No Camping signs along Mill Creek and the bus people broke camp and moved on to someplace new.

There was a trailer park just down the creek that didn't have a name but everyone called the Third World. One of the trailers was in between tenants and I made a deal with the owner to stay there for free while I sealed up the roof with trailertop and pulled all the goatheads and tumbleweeds from the yard. It was set back in a peach orchard and hidden in thickets of bamboo and shaded by big mulberry trees. The neighbors had added on plywood shacks and thatched roof verandas, and a pack of big turkeys chased off the dogs.

When I brought September into my trailer she said it was the prettiest one she'd ever seen and we could live there together and wasn't it just like being married. She stood outside on the concrete pad with the turkeys clucking around her and opened up her hand and said dude, it's starting to rain.

The raindrops fell black on the gravel and then it stopped and the sun burned down some more. There was no furniture inside, so once it got dark we spread out a sheet and lay on the floor. It was too hot to sleep or talk. We set the electric fan at our feet and sprayed water from a squirt bottle and let it mist down over us. Someday when I'm rich, said September, I'm going to take you to Spain, or maybe I'll take you to France. The floor of the trailerhouse went on forever in every direction and lying there on it we never once reached the edge.

I had a day off and September said let's drive down to see my grandmother, it's her birthday coming up. So we left early in the morning and drove south out of town out of Utah onto the reservation, through Round Rock and down to Fort Defiance. There she was, September, in the car, with me. She held my hand.

September's grandmother was four feet tall and about a hundred years old. She lived in a dirt-floor hogan where she drank rum all day with her best friend Hector who sometimes broke in at night and stole all her money. She always forgave him a few days later when he brought back a fresh bottle. She didn't speak English but looked up at me and smiled and gripped my arm with cold hard bird hands. September tried to remember a couple words in Navajo but mostly they just smiled and held hands. September said to me isn't she cool?

Then her uncle and aunt had us over to the house where I sat on the porch with Uncle Teddy and drank a Sharps. After dinner he laid out a chart of the different Navajo dances and showed me pictures and let me pick up a religious necklace and brought the kachinas out of the closet and unwrapped them from the balls of newspaper and explained everything there was to know. He was generous and kind and I knew I should be honored that he would invite me into his home and tell me about his religion and customs, but the only place I wanted to be was back with September on the floor of my trailer with the fan spinning and the cool mist floating down over us, so when Aunt Rebecca asked if we would stay the night I said I had to work the next day and we got back in the car and drove up to Utah in the darkness.

CHAPTER 12

Last Patron at
the Stuntmen's Hall of Fame

MOAB, UTAH

In 1973 stuntman and artist John Hagner brought a collection of movie knickknacks and charcoal portraits to the desert town of Palmdale, California, and founded a museum for the car-chasers and bullettakers who made stars of Burt Reynolds and Robert Redford. He moved his collection to the Mojave Airport and years later to Moab, which was still trying to recover from the uranium bust. The town council was desperate for new business, so they rented Hagner the old Mormon church on 100 East for one dollar a year. On June 25, 1988, a personal letter arrived from President Ronald Reagan, and the doors opened at the Hollywood Stuntmen's Hall of Fame Museum and Gift Shop.

I was drinking at the Rio. The summer rains were gone and the days were hot. My trailer had been rented out. Somebody had stolen Beach Philips's dome tent. And now that I'd been living inside a while, I was too spoiled to move back to the dirt.

I needed to find a cheap room. Jenny the big waitress told me she had a place I could stay.

She lived in a cottage down the street from the Stuntmen's Museum with wooden floors and a dirt yard and a sagging porch with a Chevrolet bench seat on it. I moved into the garage. It was big and dusty with a lot of broken shoptools, and at night when I set the big fan by the open door it was cool. I got a mattress and springs out of the trash bin at the Christian Thrift and set them on top of the old workbench. September said my garage was even prettier than my trailer.

Jenny had no roommates but she had a diabetic cat named Emmett who was a fine pet so long as he got his insulin shots. She'd scared some of her old roommates away by trying to mother them. They didn't want a hot dinner and they didn't want to pop caramel corn and watch movies on the couch. They thought it was creepy when Jenny carried Emmett into the parlor and in front of everyone filled a hypodermic needle and shot him up. The last one to live there packed up all his stuff, wedged a board under the doorknob, and climbed out his window. It was two days before Jenny figured out he was gone. She told me they'd had an argument over rent money, and she hated arguing over money, so if I didn't pay her anything that was fine. It seemed like a good deal to me.

The only problem was the neighbor Widow Ricketts. She had reported Jenny's landlord to the city for running an illegal bed-and-breakfast. She said there were too many tenants coming and going. To make it worse, Mrs. Ricketts woke us up at 6:30 every morning running the vacuum cleaner over the green plastic grass. And once I saw her leave the machine running and

creep up on a cinderblock to peer over the wall and spy on us. I
don't know what she was trying to see.

It was a good home in a good location. There were always
leftovers and a pitcher of lemonade in the fridge. At the end of
the block was the Hall of Fame, a big square brick building
with a shingled roof, surrounded by dozens of concrete tablets
with the autographs and bootprints of famous stuntmen. I
didn't know any of their names. Smooth river stones balanced
on upright driftlogs and rusted wagon wheels. In the driveway
sat an Eldorado the color of butter whose license plate said
STUNTZ. In the evening the curator and his wife walked down
100 East and once their groomed little poodle climbed the
porch and sniffed at Emmett.

I wasn't sure what was inside the Hall of Fame but I liked
that it was there. All summer I had thought about taking a
tour. Once I knocked on the door but nobody answered.

As summer ended, the nights got cooler. The landlord
scraped and sanded the house and repainted it with colors called
Cantaloupe and Frost and Sage. Jenny's mother overheard at the
county clerk's office that he was planning to turn it into a bed-
and-breakfast and he might not renew Jenny's lease. He also
rototilled and dug a sprinkler system and seeded the yard with
winter rye. I had liked the dirt and the peeling paint fine.

A lot was happening in Moab. Down the street in the other
direction, the corner vacant lot with all the cottonwoods was
bought by Wendy's Hamburgers. They came in with bulldozers
and in two days winched out the trees and started to dig a foun-
dation. Pretty soon they were pouring concrete. On the north
side of town ground was broken for a new waterslide and snack
bar called the Butch Cassidy Waterpark. The Westerner Grill

closed down and the old men in overalls disappeared for a week, then resurfaced at the east wall of Dave's Corner Market where just after noon the strip of shade widened enough to sit in it and drink coffee. The newspaper ran an attack on the Stuntmen's Hall of Fame, complaining that it was getting a free ride on tax-payers' property.

The river crowds thinned out. The season would be over soon and I needed something to do. There would be no work here in the winter. Maybe I could go back to California. Maybe I could find Donny Brown. I called Annabelle Brown, but instead my cousin Shapiro answered.

He was living with her now.

"We don't know where Donny is," he said. "Annabelle says she's not mad at you and you should come out to see us."

I told him that maybe I would. I thought if I showed up with some stories of my adventures, everyone who knew me in California might be impressed by what I'd become. It sounded like a good idea. I had to go someplace, it didn't matter where. I asked September if she would come with me.

"I can't go to California, dude. I'm on probation."

"I forgot," I said. "Never mind."

"I don't want you to go."

On a cool morning I walked down the sidewalk under the poplars and knocked on the door of the Hall of Fame. Nobody came. A note instructed me to try the apartment downstairs, and there I met John Hagner who unlocked the front door and ushered me in. He flicked on the lights and I paid my three dol-lars. I was the only customer.

The first item was Bill Bixby's torn shirt from *The Incredible Hulk*. The next piece was the Breakaway Chair from *They Call Me Bruce*. I walked through slowly. The Grand Junction easy-hits station poured through the speakers. I thought there might be some sort of order to the collection, but mostly it seemed just a bunch of stuff. There was Thelma's head, Louise's torso, George Hamilton's hairpiece, photos of Rin Tin Tin, and a pistol passed from John Wayne to Steve McQueen to Johnny Cash. Between the footprints of Burt Reynolds and Lee Majors hung a glossy photo of Natalie Wood holding a pale-eyed kitten. She had signed it to all stuntmen and stuntwomen. "You sure made me look good."

A large exhibit was dedicated to a Kris Kristofferson thriller filmed right in Moab. It was called *Knights* and had Kris riding a futuristic motorbike with Kathy Long, five-time World Kick-boxing Champion. The biggest section of all was about albino stuntman Dar Robinson who jumped off a Toronto skyscraper in the movie *Stick*. His high-speed jet car was on display, the one he'd used to jump the Grand Canyon. It was donated by his widow after he died on a motorcycle in the Arizona desert.

When I got back to the lobby, John Hagner told me that if I brought some friends someday he'd show us a documentary on stunts. He said he was sorry that he had to cancel the stunt show in the backyard, but the neighbors had complained to the city.

"We used to get a real crowd out there," he said.

Back at home, Jenny was in a panic. Emmett had crawled home with a broken leg. He'd been bitten by a dog in the neighborhood.

We took him to the vet and got him a cast, and when we brought him home he looked fine. He flattened his ears as Jenny stuck him with the needle. We sat on the car seat on the porch and watched him hobble around. It was warm there in the sunlight.

Then Dogcatcher George pulled up and got out of the truck. Jenny knew him pretty well because her mom had two pit bulls that were always jumping the fence and having to be captured. He climbed the front steps and said that Widow Ricketts had been overheard at the hardware store talking about poisoning the cat next door. She was leaving a bowl of antifreeze on her turf to kill little Emmett. He said there was no law against it so there was nothing he could do, but he just thought he'd warn us. Jenny thanked him and put Emmett inside.

I charged over to Mrs. Ricketts's house with my shirt off and banged on the door. When she cracked the door open I accused her of trying to kill the cat and said we wouldn't stand for it. She said of course she wouldn't poison a kitty, it was just a nasty rumor and she was sorry it had upset us. Then I said I was sorry for getting so mad, and she accepted and said she couldn't come out from behind the screen door because of her allergies, but while I was there would I bend down and gather up the cat hair that was stuck to the AstroTurf? I got on my knees and did as she told me and fifteen minutes later took home a big furball and dropped it in the trash.

Later in the afternoon I noticed the kitchen window was open and Emmett was gone. Jenny and I hadn't seen him for hours. We searched around the yard and sang his name. I peeped into Widow Ricketts's yard but didn't see anything. By dark he hadn't come home and Jenny started to cry. I told her not to worry and she rushed into the street calling for the cat. So I followed her. She went door-to-door asking the neighbors and I waited on the sidewalk. It was windy out, almost cold. Autumn was here. Nobody had seen Emmett. Jenny asked everyone but Mrs. Ricketts. She said she didn't want to, but I talked her into it. When we knocked, Mrs. Ricketts pushed open the screen door and insisted we come in for a mug of cider.

"Your kitty will be all right," she said from the kitchen. She snipped open the packages and poured in the cider mix. Jenny and I sat on a plump couch and Widow Ricketts brought us the steaming cups.

"The Lord looks out for kitties, too."

A row of framed photos stood on the end table. The TV was on.

"Chilly out," she said. "You forget it's the desert."

Jenny was still crying a bit.

"And dry too. Forty-three years and my hands still crack every summer."

"Emmett's dead," Jenny said. Now she was crying hard again, weeping.

The Widow rubbed her hands and sipped her cider. She made an old-person sucking noise when she sipped. Then she said, let's pray for the little kitty.

We held hands. Jenny's was warm and plump and Widow Ricketts's was bony and scaly and old.

"Dear God above, please deliver us the little kitty, and remove him from harm's way, and watch over all of your flock, Lord Shepherd, and keep the devil away."

That night we heard cries from behind the garage and found Emmett wedged there between two sheets of plywood. He got a shot and everything seemed all right. But in the morning an eighteen-wheeler rolled in off Main Street and parked in front of the Stuntmen's Hall of Fame. Things were not all right. I watched a frontloader dismantle the Wagon from *The Comancheros* and lift it onto the big rig. John Hagner was prying up the concrete tablets with a shovel, and he told me the news. He was moving the museum to Ariel, Washington. The Chamber up there was building a whole Old West town. That clinched it. He was going. When I went home, Widow Ricketts was vacuuming the lawn and Jenny said the landlord had called to say we had to move out.

I sat on the porch with September in the autumn sunshine. Pretty soon it would be cold. I told her that it looked like I was going to California after all. I couldn't stay here.

"How could you not love me?" she said.

"I don't not love you."

I could see the grand opening banner at Wendy's and pretty soon the Butch Cassidy Waterpark would have its lagoon filled. Sports cars with bikes on the roof zipped up and down the street. The rye grass was sprouting green from my front lawn and just then it looked like a nice place to live.

CHAPTER 13

A Big Hole
with Nothing in It

RUTH, NEVADA

My last river trip of the season was four days down Cataract Canyon with a Japanese millionaire and his friends and geisha girls. On the kitchen boat were Big Linda the chef, her assistant, a singer and a guitar player, and me.

I was the dishwasher.

Each night when we pulled up on the beach, I set up thirteen tents and two toilets. I built shower stalls and set pails of fresh water on the fire. We set up a canopy for dinner and the guests sat cross-legged underneath it at linen tablecloths and sipped Dom Pérignon and a bottle of thirty-year-old scotch. We stood at attention in our aprons with wine glasses, champagne flutes, martini glasses, beer mugs, and cocktail tumblers. Town was seventy-five miles upriver.

For the five-course meals we had only three sets of china plates, so after the salad the musicians and I kneeled at the pails and scrubbed the dishes for the soufflé. Big Linda filled my mug with red wine. She dropped a coconut-battered jumbo shrimp with raspberry sauce in my mouth. Her assistant yelled from the fire that the tenderloin was done. My boss kicked barefoot through the sand with a bowl of olives. These aren't the cal-matas, he said, they want the fucking cal-matas. He was a Vietnam vet who'd run Cataract Canyon eighteen years. He bent down and put his hand on my shoulder.

"It's no work for a white man I tell you what."

Back in Moab the trip organizer took us to the one fancy restaurant. I watched him pull aside the waiter for ten bottles of wine. I ordered the most expensive thing they had. After dinner he gave us each a plain white envelope and we walked down the street to the Rio. I would have liked to find September and take her to the bar but she wasn't old enough to go.

Debi and Emmy were on a cigarette break in the Dodge Dart. I got in the front seat with them. They were drunk. I said watch this and pulled a stack of hundreds out of the envelope. One two three wow five oh shit motherfucker eight. The girls screamed and gave me the bottle and when it was gone we ran inside. There were hundred-dollar bills up and down the bar and rows of tequila shots and all the faces were red. I threw my money at the bartender and had a drink.

The next day my head hurt. I packed up for California. But before I could leave, there were three things to do. I had to, one, return the equipment issued to me at work, and two, pick up my last paycheck. Three, I had to say good-bye to September.

The equipment to return was four straps with steel buckles and a metal first aid kit. I got to the boatyard and found that someone had taken the first aid box. That cost me fifty dollars. Somebody had pulled my timesheet from the folder, and the accountant had assumed that I didn't work there anymore and not paid me. Then I went to see September. Someone had taken her also.

We sat there in my car for a while.

"Look at my new rings," she said.

"Where did you get them?"

She said a boy's name.

"They're nice," I said. "The rings."

"Don't feel sorry for yourself," she said. "You only have to feel what you want to feel."

I tried to look emotional.

"It doesn't matter who I fuck," she said. "I still love you the most."

I told her that I was going to miss her.

"Good."

She pulled from her pocket a glob of fluorescent putty. She said here and put it in my hand. It was cool and hard.

"What is it?" I said.

"A mushroom."

"What will I do with it?"

"Don't lose it."

She kissed me on the cheek and got out of the car. I looked at the mushroom object. There were complex swirls of colors within the orange mass. The craftsmanship was excellent.

I had seven hundred dollars in hundreds and I meant to spend it quick. With this much money I was a different person. I wasn't going to think about September at all. I was fine.

I drove to Grand Junction and bought a tape player and two new tires for the station wagon. At the truckstop I bought

Willie Nelson and Merle Haggard. I went to the Mesa Mall. There was a lot of stuff I didn't have. I paid fifty dollars for sunglasses. I ate at the Chinese restaurant and went to a movie and the next morning drove west across the desert. In Eureka I sat at the bar in the Owl Club Casino and bought a burger and fries and a Budweiser. There were t-shirts on the wall that said WRANGLERS, Western Ranchers Against No Good Liberal Environmentalist Radical Shitheads. I bought one of those too.

In San Francisco, Annabelle Brown and Shapiro Brown had been smoking speed from a glass pipe all morning. When I arrived at eleven A.M. they were eager to get to a bar to settle down.

We went to the Embers Lounge on Irving Street and I lay a hundred-dollar bill on the bar. We drank a round of Bloody Marys and then another. The bartender's name was Dolly. It was a good bar. The barstools were soft and comfortable and just the right height. Everything was red velvet and carved oak. There were no windows and the only sliver of daylight came from the door propped open with a chunk of wood.

We were the only people in there. We smoked cigarettes and tapped our feet and didn't talk.

The walls were crowded with clown paintings. One clown was riding a carousel horse with a bright blue knob that set a music box tinkling when I twisted it. On the hutch behind the bar pranced 100 clown statues and figurines.

Dolly mixed a third round and told us that she and her husband had owned the bar for forty years. A lot of clowns got broke in the earthquake. She poured in horseradish, Tabasco, celery salt, and garlic vinegar.

"This ain't no snappy tom," she said.

She served the drinks with pickled string beans that floated on top like lab specimens. Annabelle Brown went to the bathroom. I went to the jukebox and punched in songs. I felt all right. The music came on. I drank a beer. I walked a circle around the barroom and back to Dolly.

"I want a matchbook, please."

She flicked a lighter and lit my cigarette.

"Yeah but do you have a matchbook with the name of the bar so I could take it with me and keep it, something to remember this by?"

She didn't have anything like that. Sounded like a liability. My cousin Shapiro Brown smoked cigarettes and watched the TV with no sound.

"It's pretty easy to follow," he said. "Surprisingly."

Dolly told me about a groundskeeper from Golden Gate Park that used to come in at noon and get creamed. Then once after lunch he dug up the lawn he'd seeded that morning. He got sacked. Nowadays the regulars stay home and drink where they won't get pulled over. Either that or they're dead or in retirement homes.

Annabelle Brown was still in the bathroom.

A bald hairy man came in, threw back a cocktail, slapped the flanks of the pinball machine. He left. Dolly's shift ended and her husband came on. Jack was an excellent bartender. He read us the weather reports from our hometowns. His hands trembled pretty bad when he poured the juice but he only spilled a little. He couldn't manage the string beans so he passed around the jar and let us grab as many as we wanted. It was a good deal.

Annabelle came out and Shapiro went in. She sat down and rapped her fingernails on the bar and bought a drink.

"Donald's in Salt Lake City," she said. "He called me. You need to go see him. See if he's all right."

Then she clutched my wrist with cold hands.

"I love him," she said. "You need to know that."

"He'll be all right. Everyone will be all right."

"Someday we'll have babies, Donald and me. We'll both grow up and stop acting like this and have a baby, then we'll be in love again."

We didn't say any more after that.

When Shapiro came out we all got in the car and Annabelle drove to Mission Street. She waited with the motor on while Shapiro and I went into the Chinese grocery that they knew about. He asked the lady for medicine. Do you have any of the medicine? She sent us back by the bananas and a man, maybe it was her husband, pulled a sheet of blue pills from his pocket. We gave him two twenties. Driving back to Annabelle's apartment, we popped open the plastic and chewed up the pills so they'd work faster.

A week or more passed.

When it was over I couldn't remember anything and all my hundreds were gone. I had $84.52. It was November. I had to go somewhere.

I left San Francisco and drove north. I tried to sleep under the redwoods but it was too dark and quiet. In the morning I drove to Trinidad Head and walked up a steep road to a jungly point above the sea. Seals were barking. On top of the hill was a marble cross erected by the Spanish in 1775. Next to that was a satellite dish. There was nothing to do or buy.

Back in the parking lot an old couple was taking pictures of each other with their dog. Another dog ran up and the lady said

Shoo! Shoo! and she flung a handful of sand but it blew right back in her face.

I took off my shoes and walked along the beach. My feet busted through the crust into the soft sand. I picked up the bleached skull of a sea gull. It was lightweight. It was nothing. It felt like nothing in my hand.

I drove some more. I was fine. On the side of the road by Bandon, a man in a straw hat was stooped over a pile of junk. I pulled over. He had bags and steel poles and a set of small rubber tires. A skinny white puppy was tied to a cable. The man's name was Joe and the dog was called Son. I opened the back of the wagon and shoved aside my sleeping bag and we put his stuff in.

Once we were driving he told me he knew some people up in Coos Bay and we could stay with them. He looked at the clock on the dash and said we'd make it for dinner. His beard was filled with grass seeds and dust and hung to his chest. What you could see of his face was burned red and wrinkled. Son slept at his feet.

"People trust you with a dog," he said and patted the puppy. Yesterday a single woman had swung a u-turn just to pick him up. "I said lady ain't you afraid of me and she said nah if you love that dog you won't harm nobody. Turned out she'd just left her man and didn't know where she was going anyways."

We drove along the bluffs. The sun was setting. The ocean was a sheet of metal.

"Just last week an old man saw me feeding Son at a gas station and gamee a damn hunnerten dollars," he said. The old man had been holding a little Pekinese, and Joe cupped his hands to show me how small it was. The old man told Joe that his wife had just died and now they wanted him to put the dog down. It was fifteen years old. Then the old man gave Joe the money. One dog-lover to another.

"What did you do with the money?" I said.

"Spennit." Joe tickled Son on the head. "Ain't that right, boy?"

I told him about my eight hundred dollars and that I'd almost spent it all.

"No matter," he said. "Easy come, easy go."

Joe was forty-one years old. He said he was from deep Georgia. He had never left his hometown until three months ago when his son got put in the detention center for fighting.

"Wanted to see the Pacific," he said. "Stood on the Golden Gate."

He directed me off the highway and through the gray streets of Coos Bay. There was mist in the trees. I was hungry and ready to stop driving.

When we got there, it was a homeless shelter. I parked the car out front and we climbed the porch. Joe introduced me to the guys standing around smoking cigarettes and the lady in the window with the clipboard.

"No beds," she said. "But you're welcome for dinner and a shower."

We signed up. The woman gave Joe a clean white towel and he took it inside. I stayed outside and played with Son on the lawn. It was dark now and a cold wind blew off the bay.

I went inside where it was warm and the TV was on and I sat with Joe and the other men. Joe's hair was still wet.

At the other table were women with children. We said a prayer and ate. There was lettuce salad and butter beans and clam chowder with toast. Two of the men at my table talked about AA and the rest of us just ate. For dessert we had fruit salad out of the can. Joe and I washed the dishes since we hadn't been there to cook, and then we sat on the sofas with the kids and adults and watched the TV.

It was a good episode and everyone laughed.

Joe and I bought a sixpack on the way out of town. We drove up a dark two-lane road looking for a place to camp but there were houses and No Trespassing signs. It was quiet and spooky. We got back on the highway and drove a while without another side road. It was hard to see anything.

Joe said he would pay for a campsite and we ended up pulling into the Umpqua Lighthouse State Park. There was nobody in the booth so we drove through. A few motor homes were parked.

We found a site surrounded by huge shrubs like a little room in the forest. Pine trees towered way above. The black-berry brush was dense and the rangers had carved tunnels from site to site and left the trimmings on the ground.

Joe trampled into the shrubs and came out with an armload of branches. He dumped them in the fire ring.

"It's a damn different world," he said. "No oak, no maple. Back home I only burn oak. I never make a pine fire."

He kicked a redwood stump hard, then jumped on it till some wood broke off, then tossed that on the heap. His propane torch made a hot sucking noise as he held it to the pile. The blackberry leaves were oily. They crackled and spit and flashed to a flame.

The whole place lit up and I felt the heat on my eyebrows. We could see each other and the station wagon and Son and the green walls around us.

Then the fire died.

Joe and I ran to the bushes and scooped up the downed branches and flung them into the ring and again the fire crackled and spit and lit the place up.

We opened the beers and I plucked some songs on the guitar. Joe said he only liked the happy songs because he couldn't get the sad ones out of his head. I didn't want anything in my head. I was fine.

When the fire darkened, Joe disappeared down the blackberry tunnel and I heard him thrash and kick and he came back and dumped a new load on the fire. He laid out his blankets on the picnic table and I dragged my sleeping bag into the pine needles and slept.

When Joe woke me it was perfectly dark.

"Let's get a move on before the rangers come 'round."

He built another tall fire and boiled a pot of water with his torch. He had a jar of instant coffee and a five-pound bag of sugar. Mine tasted like fuel and I poured it out.

We sped along the bluffs and the darkness faded to fog. We were headed to Eugene. Joe wanted to go there. He had a catalog from an environmental store in Eugene that sold things like compost bins and water-saver showerheads. He was looking to go get him a solar panel, he said. These wheels and rods he was lugging around fit together to make a cart that carried his belongings. He called it his buggy. He had a transistor radio on his buggy but he said it was boring. He needed a TV. That's what the solar panel was for. He could watch his programs while he pushed his buggy down the road.

We got to Eugene before the stores were open, so we went to the college and ate donuts in the cafeteria. Joe found half a cig-

arette on the floor and he smoked it outside. Winter was coming and the air was crisp. We tied Son to a picnic table and he
looked afraid of the people and cars.

"You inda city now, boy," Joe told him, and rubbed him
between his ears. He looked up at me. "We ain't from the city. I
never left Gilmer County till they took my boy off."

I asked where his son's mother was and he said she'd run off
early on. She'd been too young in the first place.

At nine o'clock we asked directions and followed a boulevard past car shops and furniture showrooms. I dropped him at
the environmental store. The panel he wanted cost $95. He said
he'd check into the Salvation Army to work a few days. We lifted
his crates and bags and buggy onto the sidewalk.

"What's this here?" he said. He'd found something in the
wagon under his stuff. It was September's mushroom.

"Never mind that," I said. "It's nothing."

Traffic blasted past and horns honked and Son whimpered.
Joe leaned over to his dog.

"We inda city now, boy."

I drove north across the Columbia River and up the
Olympic Peninsula to Port Townsend and across the sound to
Seattle on a wet ferry boat. There were too many trees and rainclouds and things growing. I couldn't see anything. I wanted to
get back to the desert. Then it would all be all right. I slept on
a damp dirt road, then cut inland and climbed the Snake River
to the wide open farmland around Twin Falls and coasted down
into the Nevada flats. It was good to be able to see everything

again. At the Ruth Copper Pit were signs for the Visitors' Overlook so I followed them up a hillside to a turnaround.

I got out.

As far as I could see the earth was ripped open in a dusty yellow crater. The desert was cold and the sky was dark. The wind blew.

I opened the bin for free magma samples but it was empty. I read the informational signs. They said that as a nation we are not always proud of everything that occurred in the past. We used to not let black people vote and we used to put Japanese people in concentration camps, and until 1978 we strip-mined for copper. There's 501 pounds of copper in every U.S. home and 49 pounds in every car. I read the visitors' log.

A big hole. Impressive. Thanks.
Fucking abomination.
Wow! Inspiring.
My mom likes it but I think it's dum.
What hath man wrought?

It started to snow. Hard dry snowflakes whipped in the wind. This was where I had arrived. A big empty hole. Now I had to go somewhere else.

I drove to Utah. Donny Brown was in Salt Lake and September was in Moab. I headed to Moab. I would be all right once I got there. It was dark when I stopped in Salina for a hamburger. The pass was icy and there had been two collisions. I didn't have chains but I kept going. I was not going to stop. I sped over the Fishlake Mountains and down into the desert where there was black sky and bright stars and a flat sheet of snow.

In Moab I met September at her house and she got into my station wagon. Her teeth were small and straight. She said she was changed but she looked the same to me.

"You can't stay with me," she said. "There's not room."

"Let's get a motel," I said.

Everything was fine at the Prospector Lodge on 100 West. There was a dim lamp in the corner that we left on all night, and while she slept came the first winter freeze. I woke her in the morning and the leaves had dropped together and spread out like a blanket on the street. I wiped the moisture from the glass and when we looked out the window the snowflakes were black and the trees were desperate and the bare branches shivered in the wind. Then September told me she was not the same as she was before. She loved me but everyone needed to be on their own trip.

I'm not on a trip, I said.

Yes you are.

Can I be on your trip?

No.

I took her home and left Moab for Salt Lake City.

PART
THREE

CHAPTER 14

This Is the Place

SALT LAKE CITY, UTAH

In 1823 a seventeen-year-old boy in the frontier town of Palmyra, New York, was visited by an angel. The spirit called itself Moroni and whispered to the boy of sacred golden tablets from an ancient people, buried in the woods not far away. But when the boy went to the site, it was protected by a large toad who turned into a man and conked the boy on the head.

Four years later, after much digging and searching, young Joseph Smith announced to his family and bride that he had discovered the written history of a lost tribe of Israel. Inscribed on the golden plates he'd unearthed was the wondrous tale of two sons of Lehi who had settled America centuries before and whose descendants had evolved into warring races, the fair-skinned Nephites and the red-skinned Lamanites. For a thousand years they fought until the good Nephites were driven to extinction. In their final days, their prophet Mormon wrote down the history of his people and buried it in the woods that would one day become upstate New York.

Of course nobody believed Joseph Smith's story. Towns-

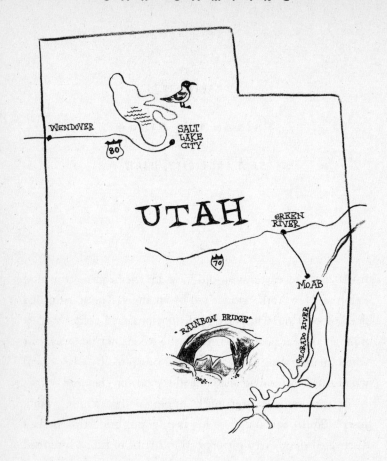

people broke into his house and smashed open the chest where he kept the tablets. When they revealed the chest to be empty, they denounced him as a fraud. But as if by miracle, Joseph had removed the golden tablets the night before and hurried them to a safer place, which in itself was another miracle because each of the bricks of gold weighed about two hundred pounds.

Joseph set about translating the ancient script from a language he called reformed Egyptian into modern English. With his wife as his scribe, he sat in the parlor with the tablets covered in a linen tablecloth. Naturally his family wanted to see the golden treasures but Joseph assured them that to lay eyes upon the holy scripts would bring instant death. So Joseph translated the Egyptian characters without actually looking at them, a feat made possible only with the help of the magic rocks named Urim and Thummim that came with the tablets. With Moroni at his shoulder Joseph stared into the rocks and the words came to him.

"I, Nephi," he began, "having been born of goodly parents . . ."

His Book of Mormon was a hit. It was read in the frontier states, loved by some and burned by others. By the second edition, Joseph had changed his title on the front page from author to translator and soon he declared himself Prophet and Founder of the new Church of Jesus Christ of Latter-day Saints.

For the next twenty years Joseph Smith and his brethren moved from state to state in search of a homeland. They were driven from New York and Ohio and Illinois and Missouri by mobs of Gentiles until finally in 1844, as a way to stop the persecution of his followers, Joseph Smith let himself be arrested for treason in Carthage, Illinois. As he waited in jail the state militia arrived with bayonets and blackface and opened fire on the cell. Wounded, Joseph leapt from the second story window to the street where the jeering mob dragged him onto a curb and fired four shots to his chest. Just as one of the murderers stepped forward with a knife to cut off the dead prophet's head, the clouds parted and God's holy sun shone down. The Gentiles dropped their weapons and ran away. Joseph Smith was a martyr.

The Mormons were now saved. They had more reason than

ever to clear out of America and start their own Holy Land in the desert. They wanted to get to nowhere, or at least the Mexican territory, and carve out their own country like the Texans had done. A new prophet stepped forward, a man like Moses who would lead the tribe to the Promised Land. In 1847 he led the Saints from their camps in Nebraska and Iowa out into the wilderness. He pioneered a trail to the westernmost Rocky Mountain range, and looking down from Big Mountain onto the Salt Lake Valley and the desert beyond it, looking down upon the State of Deseret, upon Israel, he turned to his people and staked his immortal claim.

"This is the place," said the Prophet Brigham Young, and they knew then that they had found their home.

I called Donny Brown from a payphone in Green River and he gave me his address in Salt Lake City. He said that he had an apartment and was having trouble making the rent, so if I didn't have anything else to do I could move in. We didn't have much else to say and then the three minutes were up.

An apartment sounded like a good idea. It was cold out now and I needed a place indoors to stay put. Soon September would change her mind about me and meanwhile a big city would have money to make and women to meet. It would keep me from thinking too much. Driving up the coal canyons near Price it sounded like a good plan. The wind whipped into the Subaru through the gaps around the windshield and I pulled my ski cap down the back of my neck.

I followed Donny's directions through Salt Lake City to 228 East First Avenue on the top of a hill. I could see the Mormon temple downtown and the sun sinking behind it and the sky all purple. The snow glowed orange on the mountains behind me. Donny Brown came out of the gray brick building and kicked through the slush on the sidewalk.

"It's the oldest apartment in the city," he said. We carried my stuff in from the station wagon. He had on coveralls with a Hudson General patch on the pocket for his job handling luggage at the airport. He didn't look like a Bad Man. He looked old. We'd known each other a long time.

"Clean and serene," said Donny Brown. "Sixty days now."

On the stoop, a one-armed man finished a cigarette and dropped it in a coffee can full of butts. Water dripped from icicles on the fire escape.

Donny had the front room of the first floor. It was long and humid and smelled like fried meat and you could hear the hiss of the radiator. The wet heat made the floorboards warp. The ceiling was high and the wood trim was stained black.

I asked Donny Brown where he'd been all those months and he said a lot of it he couldn't remember. I asked if he was still living in the Right Now, and he said sort of. Now he was living One Day at a Time. He slid the window open and the cold air blew in. He lit a cigarette.

"I'm just a man," he said. "Nothing more."

He was serious. I decided to change the subject.

"The good thing about a city," I said, "is the money and the women."

"Yeah," said Donny Brown. He poured some coffee grounds into a tin pot.

"Two guys like us," I said.

"Want some of this?"

Donny Brown and I sat on the couch and he drank his coffee and smoked a cigarette and I had a cup of water. I told him that I had a girlfriend in Moab and that as soon as she turned eighteen and her probation ended she would come up to visit me. He didn't say anything to that. It was hard to impress Donny Brown.

The door knocked and it was the neighbor and her little boy. She was white and he was black.

"Can I run the hose through your window?" she said. "My waterbed leaked out again."

Donny said okay and she went outside to do it.

"She does this pretty often," said Donny. "Her husband's white too, in case you were wondering."

The nozzle of the hose poked in the window overhead and the neighbor's voice called out. Donny Brown tugged the hose across the apartment and handed it to her in the hallway and closed the door as far as it would go.

"You meet a lot of women in Salt Lake?" I said.

"Just Shania." He motioned at the garden hose. "She's the only one."

Donny Brown said that Shania lived across the hall and was nineteen and three months pregnant. Every time her husband beat her up she ran to Donny's room to call her mom on his phone. He thought maybe his was the only telephone in the building. One night while he was trying to sleep she sat on his mattress and cried and told her mom that she wanted to move back home but that she had to hang up now because if her husband found her in the neighbor's apartment he'd shoot them both. Then she stayed on the phone for another twenty minutes.

"After that I bought a .22," said Donny Brown. "I got a

pretty good deal at the pawnshop. It's under the mattress if you want to see it."

After Shania was done with the hose, Donny went to the kitchen and plopped a handful of ground moose in a sizzling pan and dumped in a jar of tomato sauce. He had a cousin on his dad's side who lived in Layton and was a hunter. Donny Brown had twenty pounds of moose meat in the freezer.

"It's a bit gamy," he said when we ate the spaghetti. Then he opened the windows and let in the cold air. The boiler wouldn't turn down and even though it was snowing out it was eighty degrees and muggy inside. Donny Brown held his cigarette out the window while he smoked it. He didn't smile or make any expression. He was not like he used to be.

"Easy does it," he said.

Nobody likes to sleep two men in a bed. But the couch was short and the floor was crowded, so that night I got in my sleeping bag on the mattress next to Donny Brown. It wasn't much different than camping out in a tent. I went right to sleep but I think Donny just lay there. He woke me up accidentally when he crawled out and went into the kitchen and I heard him making coffee. Then later I woke up again when I felt his arm draped over me. He was asleep and I could hear him grinding his teeth. It was a strange place for him to put his arm but I figured it was all right because he was my cousin and he'd had a tough year. Pretty soon I fell asleep too.

In the morning Donny Brown was up at 6:30 brushing his teeth loudly and was out the door for the airport. I sat at the table and drank a cup of water from the tap. Donny had gone from rock singer with a rich wife to baggage handler living with his cousin. Now we were both failures. I didn't feel so embarrassed about getting a job. I picked up the newspaper he'd left behind. There was an ad for a construction job paying five dollars an hour so I drove down to the site on 700 South.

"My name's Carter," said the foreman. "You got a good pair of boots?"

I showed him.

"Those'll do, but if you last a while you'll want a steel shank."

Carter and I lifted rolls of pink fiberglass insulation out of the truck and I crawled under the house and lay on my back and stuffed the foam up between the joists. I squirmed around down there until lunchtime then went back in the afternoon with a sheet of plastic and a staple hammer. It was hard to pound in the staples because there wasn't room to swing my arm. That night I was sore and I lay on the mattress in my sleeping bag and thought about how long it would take to save enough money to buy a truck. The toilet wheezed and gurgled in the other room. Shania's son cried through the walls and she hollered at him.

"Your hair will never be straight!

"Your hair will never be straight!"

In the pioneer days, the Mormons didn't believe in money. Everyone worked hard and helped each other and got the same amount of food and supplies. It took everyone's cooperation just to survive in the desert. But once they tamed nature, they saw how much good stuff they could get if they had a job and made more money. Carter told me that now the Latter-day Saints own the biggest cattle ranch in the world and most of the stock in Pepsi-Cola.

There were four of us on the crew. Everyone was blond and except for me everyone was Mormon. Augie was the boss but he usually left Carter in charge of Rob and me. On the job they talked about God and the meaning of life. I liked it because on the painting crews I had worked before the only talk was pussy pussy smoke pussy. When Augie came back from a church cruise of the Caribbean he told us that when he and his wife visited the Mayan temples the guide proved that everything in the Book of Mormon was true.

"I got chills down my spine," he said. "Margo was weeping, really weeping."

Augie said he gave twenty-five percent of his income to the church and asked what the others gave. Rob and his wife didn't give anything. They hardly went to church. Carter said on a good month he gave ten percent. He was twenty-seven and married, had four kids and could build a house by himself. He made thirteen dollars an hour. Augie told him to give to the church no matter what. Rob told him to heck with the church, he should pay the rent.

But I didn't think Carter cared about the church or the rent. When Rob and Augie went up on the roof, I asked him what he'd do if he got a thousand dollars and he said buy a couple rifles or maybe make a down payment on a snowmobile.

Friday was payday, and Augie took us to Chuck-A-Rama at noon. His treat. All four of us got in the truck. I liked driving around the wide city streets in the crewcab with my jeans and boots powdered in drywall dust. We sat at a booth and I scraped clean a plate of roast beef and mashed potatoes and chicken wings. We drank a pitcher of root beer.

Augie told me about the company. He had a contractor's license and a realtor's license, and he bought abandoned and condemned houses and fixed them up till they were like new then sold them.

"If you ever want to make it in this business," he said when he passed around the paychecks, "every payday, go buy a tool. Once you get the tools you can work for yourself."

So in the evening I cashed my check and drove down State Street in my work clothes. In the pawn shops I got a tool belt and pliers and a tape measure and taping knives. At Sears I bought a fiberglass framing hammer and took it home and brought it inside and twirled it around while I sat on the couch. I liked the way it felt in my hand.

Things were dull. Donny and I worked. At Christmas we went to Donny's relatives' house. They gave him a used miniature TV set. They gave me a windbreaker. His cousin took us out on snowmobiles. The cousin's machine was a lot faster than ours and he left us behind. We ended up sinking into the deep snow and having to push the thing back to the road.

On New Year's Eve we turned on the television. The screen was only three inches wide, black-and-white, so we had to sit close at the table.

"Want to watch a little TV?" said Donny Brown. "Get it? A little TV."

It was a pretty funny joke.

"Let's watch a little TV," I said.

Carter and I started a new job off Sixth North. It was a con-demned old two-bedroom that had been boarded up for seven years since the old man died. Carter said the Tongans were mov-ing into the neighborhood but I didn't see any. The junk man had taken four days to haul out the rotted furniture and soot-covered piles of garbage. He found seventeen dead cats and a dog.

"There was also a stack of dirty books," said the junk man. "And a dil-doo."

Carter pried the plywood off the back door and my eyes watered. The smell of cat piss was like hot mist. We had to get at the pipes and wires under the house, but neither of us wanted to crawl around down there, so Carter got out the wormdrive and cut out a trap door. Stretched out in the dirt were the dried-up bodies of more dead cats.

"My heck," said Carter. "My hell."

We took turns heaving the cats onto the trash pile in the backyard. In the bathroom were preserved bottles of cough syrup and aftershave. Carter and I took out our hammers and swung at the medicine chest until the mirror and the glass bot-tles were smashed in shards on the floor.

"Tongan house," he said.

We brought bag lunches and when it was time sat in our separate cars and ate. The sun warmed me through the wind-shield. Carter was in his van almost two hours.

"I musta got caught up in my book," he said when we went back to work. He told me about the story he'd read in the Book of Mormon with people killing and stabbing and carrying on. Then he switched the radio from classic rock to the soft country station.

"I guess I shouldn't have anything against the Tongans," he said. "It says we're all God's children and all that."

We filled the airless sprayer with Lysol and coated the place twice but the next day it still smelled like piss. We bought ten gallons of mistints and sprayed the walls and ceilings and floors.

"That oughta seal that smell in," said Carter, looking up at the sky. "A cold front's blowing in."

In the morning when we pried the frosted plywood off the door, the house still stank. We put on our particle masks, which looked like they'd help but didn't. Our eyes burned. It was cold and we worked in our coats and gloves and hats. There was no heater. The old man had burned coal all his life and never had the gas hooked up.

He had also hidden five hundred empty mason jars under the living room floor. We cut open a trapdoor and set a trash can outside the big window frame and played basketball.

Crash crash crash went the mason jars.

"What do you think he did with the jars?" I said.

"Probably something perverted."

A little boy with a sad girlish face appeared on the windowsill and watched us. We stopped throwing.

"Smells like pee," he said.

I tossed a couple jars past him and they smashed into the trash can.

"Why are you breaking those bottles?" he said.

"They're not bottles, they're jars," said Carter. "Where's your mama?"

"She's asleep," he said. "I'm allowed over here but my sister's not."

A while later the mother came out in bare feet and a night-gown, her hair dyed black and eyes bloodshot. She was about my age. She was pretty.

"Come on home," she said to her son. Then she looked at us. "Brr. Cold."

Once she was gone, Carter smashed a jar with his hammer. "Whore," he said.

Winter was almost over. The streets were muddy. With the thaw, the smell of moose meat in the apartment got stronger. Dark brown something bled out of the kitchen faucet. I bought a mattress at Deseret Industries and laid it on the floor and we hung a sheet from the ceiling to divide Donny's side and mine. The room got smaller.

Donny Brown got home from work before me and got the first bath. When my turn came I had to wipe the film from the tub. There was no shower and when the boiler crapped out there was no hot water.

In the evenings when Donny was at his meetings I stayed home and lay on the couch and looked at the ceiling. I tried to call September, but her mom told me she'd moved out. She'd been arrested for not paying her speeding tickets and now she was living in a school bus with her friend Beach Philips.

"I know him," I said. I wondered why she wanted to live with Beach Philips.

"He was nice enough to get her out of jail," said her mom. When I asked if there was any way to reach September she said if she saw her she'd give her the message to call.

The money and the women in Salt Lake City were not what I'd hoped for. When I wasn't working I lay on the couch and read the used truck ads in the classified section and thought about which one I might buy someday. Or I just daydreamed about September and the desert and waited for something to happen. I broke up time into the smallest increments possible, smaller than a millisecond, and then I tried to add them up. Then I would wonder if in my tally I should include time spent counting time or just time spent experiencing time, and then I would lose track and pretty soon I couldn't tell if time was moving forward or backward. I couldn't tell the difference between living in the Right Now and living One Day at a Time. When Donny Brown came home I was still lying there waiting for something to make sense or for anything to happen. Finally one night the phone rang but instead of September it was Annabelle Brown.

"It's so good to hear your voice," she said. She was about to cry. "You sound great."

In the other room the toilet made a noise.

"You too," I said. "I'll get Donny."

I went out to the stoop so they could talk. Shania and her husband were carrying a cot into a pickup truck. They were moving to a house. Shania patted her stomach.

"It's a girl," she said. She showed me her stroller and called it a perambulator.

"Don't you love that word?" she said. "Perambulate?"

"Hey, yeah."

"Shanny, get in the car," said her husband.

"It's a truck," she said. "Dummy."

When I went back in, Donny Brown told me that Annabelle

was flying out to visit. She was ready to work with him to patch things up. He had told her he didn't want to, but she'd insisted. She'd already bought a plane ticket. She would be here in one week.

Donny Brown said it would be good if I could get out of town for the weekend. That sounded like a good idea. I was getting tired of the couch and the days were sunny. I said maybe I'd go out to the West Desert.

"What's there?" said Donny Brown.

"Nothing."

The week passed quickly because I was thinking about the desert. Winter was over. I was going camping again. On Friday, Carter and I wanted to go to Sizzler instead of Chuck-A-Rama for payday lunch. Augie didn't show up at noon so we put down our tools and waited for him. I went to the house next door and asked for a glass of water. The pretty girl with the girlish son rubbed her eyes and asked what time is it and went to the sink. I thanked her and drank the water and set the glass by the screen door.

We were still waiting for Augie when someone drove up in a Monte Carlo. The tailpipe scraped as he pulled into the driveway. Carter introduced Tweedy. He used to work for Augie.

"It's my Scottish name," said Tweedy getting out of the car. "It's on the family coat of arms."

Tweedy had a brand-new air compressor in the trunk.

"It's totally legit," he said. "I could show you the papers."

He also had some fancy speakers and golf clubs he could get out of pawn if we were interested. He said as soon as he was flush he was going to get his electric guitar back and start rehearsing with his band. They were a cross between gothic and death metal. Tweedy had long hair.

Then the neighbor's screen door swung open and the water glass rolled down the stairs and broke. The mother said fuck, pulled back her hair, and went inside.

"I know that bitch," Tweedy said. He slapped the back window of the Monte Carlo. "She works at the titty bar on State Street. My buddy fucked her."

Augie pulled up in the crewcab.

"What you got for me, Tweedy?" he said. He got out and ran his hands over the air compressor. "Can't use it."

Augie turned to Carter and me.

"Chuck-A-Rama?"

But we told him the Sizzler.

"Sizzler it is," said Augie. "But you got a five-buck limit."

We all loaded our plates at the buffet, and while we ate we talked about injuries we'd had and car accidents we'd seen. Carter's father-in-law worked at the Kennicot open pit mine and he'd seen a man drenched in molten copper and cooked alive. I went back to the lunch bar and got a plateful of little corn ears and scampi.

Carter had another story. This guy his father-in-law knew worked at a train yard and one day he got his torso pinched between two freight cars. He didn't bleed, he couldn't even feel it, but his body was compacted between the massive ball and socket. The doctor said that there was no choice but to pull apart the cars, but there was no saying what would happen. The guy was totally conscious and alive. They brought in his wife and she was led through the crowd and they had everyone back off and give them a moment alone. Then with an ambulance standing by, the train cars pulled apart. The man collapsed and bled to death in sixty seconds.

"I wouldn't want my wife to watch me die," said Carter.

"If anyone wants a refill," Augie said, standing up and rattling the ice in his cup, "get it now."

Before I left work that night I went to the neighbor's porch and picked up the broken glass. It was dark now and I knew she couldn't see me. I stood by the window. The TV was on and it flickered behind the curtain. Her kids were in there. I could hear her setting the table and taking a lid off a pot. I imagined she was serving canned soup in her underwear, maybe wearing a silk robe. It was cold standing on the porch. I could have stayed the whole night there wondering what she was doing inside, trying to get a look between the curtains. I was the same as everybody else.

She must have seen my shadow because the door swung open and there she was. She had all her clothes on. I was standing there with a handful of glass and I held it out.

"I picked this up for you," I said.

She said thanks and it was nice of me. We looked at each other. She had been crying. She took the glass and went back inside.

When I got home that night Donny Brown was sitting on the couch clenching his fists. Annabelle was arriving the next day at noon. Donny had tried to get the day off but they wouldn't let him have it. He said he might just quit. I gathered my camping stuff into a pile while Donny looked at the little TV. At eleven P.M. a man came to the door. He wore no shirt and camouflage cutoffs. I think he might have lived upstairs. He wanted to know what time it was and if he could use the phone. Donny slammed the door.

"All I want is for everybody to leave me alone," he said.

Then in the morning the man knocked again. He was drunk. He asked for money.

"My kids are crying and I need to get them some milk."

Donny kicked the door closed and said these people these people these fucking people.

The plane landed at noon. Annabelle was here to fix the marriage. But when her flight arrived, Donny Brown was not there to meet his wife. Instead he was in the station wagon with me heading east out of Lehi toward the West Desert. We were going camping. Out past Fairfield the land was flat and we pulled onto a dirt road. It was like old times. Me and Donny in the car not saying very much.

The West Desert was a barren place. It had been raining and the ground was green, but there were no features. It was spring. Long slopes of rock and gravel were dotted with shrub junipers. Now and then we saw a mobile home down some double-track road at a sheep camp. There were no other people.

"It's empty out here," said Donny Brown. "It's empty empty empty."

Finally we found a wide flat place and parked. It was clear and cold. Donny had his .22 pistol so we fired some shots into the hillside.

We walked up a ridge toward a satellite dish and the first thing I saw was a sheep carcass. The flesh had been pecked away and the bones were clean and white in a nest of yellow fleece. I looked away and saw a pronghorn down on the flats. He watched us then made a sound like a duck and bounded off.

We kept walking up the hillside. It was steeper than it had looked from the car, and loose, and I was out of breath. At the top was the radio transmitter or whatever it was. A fence around it said No Trespassing. Donny Brown fired the gun in there but didn't hit anything.

The hilltop was long and flat and I kept walking to see if there was anything else up there. Donny was shooting at other things.

In a juniper tree I saw a big beetle suspended between branches. I looked closer. It was petrified and hairy, long since dead, preserved.

Deeper inside the tree, I saw a burlap bag tied to a limb. I pulled it off and set it on the ground.

There was something inside.

I pinched the bottom of the bag and jerked it, and out rolled some little green bodies. They were hard and dead and hairless and their faces were dried up and eyes scrunched tight and their arms twisted outward double-jointed.

It was a bag of puppies. I pressed one with my foot and it was hard and fragile like a lightbulb.

It was the tallest tree around, the one I'd found, six feet tall, half a mile from the nearest road. Who knows how long they'd hung there, and who knows whose they were?

"Donny, come here," I said and kicked the puppies into a line. And before I could turn around he said spread them out farther and loading his gun he was ready to shoot.

CHAPTER 15

Historical Tour at the Butterfield Southern

COCHISE STRONGHOLD, ARIZONA

Communing with nature is the last resort of a desperate person. Just look at Thomas Jeffords. In 1856 the redheaded steamship captain quit a good navy job on the Mississippi River and headed west to dig gold from the hills of New Mexico. He learned every ditch, drainage and hoodoo between Santa Fe and Tucson. When the Civil War broke out, he joined the Union Army as a scout and served in the battle of Val Verde. He ran papers back and forth through Apache country while all around settlers were killed dead in their saddles by the arrows and battle axes of the Chiricahua. He knew his way around.

When the Civil War ended, Thomas Jeffords quit the army and wandered into the desert. He wanted to get to nowhere. By day he ambled through the dust with a burro and a pickaxe, and by night lay out in the rice grass and looked at the stars. But the war between the Indians and the whites raged on. Back in Tucson, the settlers were under siege. One in three mail carriers was killed by the Apache. In 1872 Thomas Jeffords got sick of nowhere and slipped into the Tucson Pueblo where he was hired to deliver the mail.

He did things differently than other settlers. He watched the smoke signals. He learned to speak Apache. Striking out from Tucson he fanned a smoky campfire and floated signals into the desert sky. He plodded up wide open washes in plain view of the invisible Apache and trekked into the Cochise Stronghold from which no white man had ever returned.

When I struck out from Salt Lake City to Arizona I didn't know what the Stronghold was. I'd never heard of Cochise or Thomas Jeffords. I'd quit my job with the Mormons and told Donny Brown I was moving out.

Donny didn't react much. After quitting his airport job, he was working for a drywaller. He came home at night with his face covered in white dust. He looked sick. If he ever found out what had happened to Annabelle he didn't say so to me. He never said anything about her.

When my cousin asked why I was leaving, I didn't know what to say. The real reason I had to go was that lying on the sofa all those days watching the ceiling and spying on the clock, I'd suspected I was coming undone and thought I should do something about it. I had reread Young Tom's list of dos and don'ts and decided I should not Have Make-Believe Conversations but I should Take Walks Outside and Commune with Nature. Of course I didn't want to say so to Donny Brown because he would have known I was cracking. I couldn't tell him I was trying to get to nowhere. Neither did I want to tell him that I wanted to go back to Moab for September. It was important to never admit that thinking about her made my stomach clench, because that would knock down the walls and she would pour in from all sides. So instead of telling the truth, I made something up.

"I'm dropping into the desert," I said. "I'll have an adventure."

He asked where I was going.

I wished I had some place to tell him but I couldn't think of one.

"You should check out Cochise Stronghold," he said. "I went down there when I still thought I might be an Indian. It's pretty."

I found it on the map and drove all day and most of the night to Tucson. In the morning Interstate 10 took me east past Benson.

It was March and a good day to drive through the desert. The big dusty flats were a sponge after yesterday's rain and everything was crisp and bright and still. I cracked the window and the blast of cold air smelled like wet sagebrush.

On my lap lay a brand new dingo dog called Tuffy. That was the name it had come with. I had acquired the thing from a cardboard box at a gas station on the Navajo Reservation. It had looked useless sitting alone in the box with its splotches of white, beige, and blue-gray, and its big black eyes like it had been punched. It was the last one the boy had to get rid of, and he seemed a bit impatient. I was worried what he might do with it if I didn't take it.

Then all of a sudden I saw that if I had a dog I would have a reason to take walks outside and commune with nature and nobody would think there was something wrong with me, so I scooped it up and took it away.

Within five minutes of having it, a man told me it was the homeliest mutt he'd ever seen, but since then it hadn't done much but sleep on my lap. Now the dog stood up and blinked and yawned and paced the passenger seat. I didn't know what it wanted. I was afraid of it.

Approaching the Stronghold I realized that my torn-up road atlas was not very detailed. It showed my destination a few miles south of the highway but showed no roads leading into it.

I got off the Interstate at Dragoon and drove through the village of knocked-down pioneer shacks and silver-topped trailer homes. Except for the woman in a blue uniform loading parcels onto a truck at the post office, Dragoon was as still as the scoops of rock on the horizon.

I zipped around a bend and was back on a straight even two-lane with no buildings or people or signs. I pulled into the first driveway and wondered where to go. Spanning the dirt road before me was a sign that read Flying Horseshoe Ranch and Curios Shop. Free Historical Tours.

Here I was. Whenever I thought I was nowhere I always ended up some place like this where there were already people. It's all been touched. But now that I was lost I didn't mind. Maybe these people could help me. I put the dog down in the dirt and it pooped and peed. That made me feel kind of important, like I'd done something right.

I bumped past dried-up fields and corrals and now Tuffy climbed my leg to sniff the fresh air, so I held it out the window as we drove and it seemed to like it all right. We reached a dusty compound of barns, sheds, garages and dwellings where I killed the motor alongside a trailer. A pair of pony-size Airedales loped across the yard and sniffed me and my dog as we got out of the station wagon.

Behind the main house an old man in a plaid coat and an orange hunting cap stooped over a grinding wheel. Each time he leaned into it, the machine howled and coughed up sparks onto the weeds.

A paper sign on the door of the trailer instructed me to Ring Doorbell, so I poked the tin button and right away a woman descended the back steps of the house and tapped the man's shoulder. The grinder whined to a stop. He drew back a creaking section of wire fence then dragged a lame leg through the gravel and dust.

"Clifton Comstock," he said. "I left my microphones in the house so I didn't hear you buzz."

We climbed up to the landing and he ushered me into the trailer. My dog couldn't make it up the stairs so I left her down there. The big Airedales seemed pretty friendly.

The lights in the trailer flickered on and an electric heater whirred. On the walls hung watercolor desertscapes, Indian sand paintings, barnwood clocks. The shelves held meteorites and dinosaur bones, and a petrified stump sat on the floor. Little cardboard boxes brimmed with arrowheads and polished stones.

"You'll have to talk loud because I don't have my microphones."

"I haven't said anything yet."

"Say again?" He cupped his hand over his ear and peered my way. His eyes filled the entire lenses of his glasses.

"I'm looking for Cochise Stronghold," I said.

"Sometimes I'll take a tour of the Butterfield Swing Station," he said. "It's on my property here, but not today, it's too cold out and my fingers will ache."

"Can you give me directions?"

"Oh yes that's easy. You just walk out back here past the sheep pen and the pond and head out toward the mill. Most people find it."

"Cochise Stronghold is just out back?"

"Now why did you want to see the Stronghold?"

"Someone told me to." I said. "I'm just driving through."

"The Butterfield is more historical," he said. "Must be two years now since I found the site where Cochise met with General Howard. Of course Thomas Jeffords brought the general to the spot. The spring is run dry and nobody goes up there but me and so when I found that buckboard axle I figured it must be the place. We had the historical society and the national parks and the rangers come down and they put up a plaque."

We talked awhile, then went back outside so he could give me directions.

"See that oak in the ravine? Head past it in a straight line. Follow the cow trail along the buried pipeline and the ruins are on your right. If you reach the windmill, turn around because you went too far."

Then he looked down at Tuffy.

"You're taking that dog with you?"

"I think so."

"That's a good dog," he said. "That dog'll run circles around you to scare off the snakes."

I whistled and Tuffy actually followed me.

"Some people go up there and don't find it," Comstock called after me. "You'll find it."

We kicked through a red dirt cow pasture and ducked under barbed wire on the way to the Butterfield Swing Station and Mail Stop, whatever that was. It didn't matter where we were going. Tuffy didn't run any circles but she did keep up.

Clifton Comstock had told me that he had traveled to Craig, Colorado, in 1931 to drive horses back to his home in Pennsylvania. He was sixteen. For years he roamed the West, traded horses and stock. Comstock told me that he was in Death Valley with Scotty before Scotty even built his castle.

He moved to Dragoon in 1959 and had been raising sheep on the Flying Horseshoe ever since. He was known in southeastern Arizona for ranching Japanese fallow deer, Norwegian reindeer, even zedonks. He said if I was lucky I might run across Strauss, whose father was a donkey and mother a zebra.

After we'd walked a mile through the sagebrush, we reached the rickety wooden windmill with an irrigation canal flowing underneath. We'd gone too far. The dog went to get a drink and slipped in the water and as it tried to claw its way to land was swept downstream. It was a slow current and I didn't have to walk too fast to keep up with the dog as it floated along and whimpered. There was a flat spot where it could have easily got ashore but the stupid thing paddled to the wrong side of the creek and tried to climb a mud bank. I watched it for a few minutes then got impatient and jumped across the water and pulled it out. The last thing I needed from that animal was a hassle.

The dog was shivering so I dried it on my jacket sleeves then put it inside against my stomach. Tuffy seemed grateful to be in there with me. She was the first thing I had ever rescued.

The Butterfield Station was a one-room building collapsed to a jumble of granite blocks enclosed by cattle fence. Three slanted crosses poked up from the red dirt.

The Dragoon station was built by the Butterfield Southern Overland Mail Company, which ran stagecoaches between St. Louis and San Francisco. In the 1850s settlers made peace with Cochise and his Chiricahua Apache, allowing coaches to cross the Dragoon Mountains undisturbed. The swing station provided fresh supplies and horses along the four-week journey.

Then in 1860 a young lieutenant from the U.S. Cavalry captured six of Cochise's warriors, including his brother, and demanded that the chief confess to a kidnapping he had not done. Cochise was crazy with rage and stormed the Apache Pass Butterfield Station and killed three white-eyes. The lieutenant hanged the six innocent Chiricahua.

Nobody was ready for the storm that erupted. Cochise mourned alone for twenty-one days. He was getting old but he was still the most feared chief in the territory. He summoned his warriors.

"There will be ten white-eyes slain for every Chiricahua slain. This I pledge."

The blood spilled. With the U.S. Army called back east for the Civil War, the Arizona Yankees huddled for safety inside the high walls of Tucson Pueblo. Customers riding the Butterfield Southern were ambushed and murdered. The trail and its stations were abandoned.

Back at the curio shop, I found Clifton Comstock entertaining some pudgy midwesterners who were wintering in the desert. He knew them by name and it was clear that they came in every year to see the ranch and purchase tchotchkes.

I handled the belt buckles and read the news clippings on the wall. Matted behind glass was an 1872 article from the *Washington Daily Morning Chronicle.* The author was General Oliver Otis Howard, sent by President Grant to make peace with the Apache. He was an evangelical Christian who hoped to save some souls as well as lives. Just up from the Butterfield Station in the shady glen at Dragoon Springs, Howard and Cochise had signed a treaty.

"That I found folded up in an old book," said Comstock. "Of course I buy old books. Collect them."

The Iowans had left. I had his attention.

"You'll see that Howard talks about crossing a stream at the springs. That'll throw some people off because there's no water now." Comstock told me that the springs had dried up after the earthquake of 1888, and the ranchers and cowboys who knew where it was all died off, and soon enough the place was forgotten. Then in 1994, 122 years after the peace was made, Comstock was driving cattle up the draw and found an old wagon axle.

"This is it, I said to myself. If they could get a buggy in here, that meant that was where the road came through."

Clifton Comstock had found the site of the historical treaty signing.

I spent some money and left with photos, articles, a brass belt buckle in the shape of a Kenworth sleepercab and vague directions to Cochise Stronghold. I got back on the two-lane blacktop and drove east. Tuffy was warm and dry now and I set her on the dashboard so she could see. At the second farm I made a right onto an unmarked road that forked twice, turned to dirt, and was marked with occasional signs for the Stronghold.

The treaty had been signed by Cochise and Howard, but the real peacemaker was the riverboat captain Thomas Jeffords. He was the only white man who had befriended the warlord Cochise. They smoked a pipe together. Legend says they slit their palms and bound their hands and became blood brothers. It sounded to me like the kind of legend that somebody made up. And then when President Grant wanted peace with the Chiricahua, it was Jeffords who arranged the meeting at Dragoon Springs.

"Hereafter," said Cochise, "the white man and the Indian are to drink the same water, eat of the same bread, and be at peace."

Legend also says that before the treaty, Thomas Jeffords fell in love with a Chiricahua maiden and married her in a tribal ceremony. They were happy until his wife was killed in a shoot-out with the U.S. Cavalry. These legends try to tell you that for a white man the most advanced way of communing with nature is to marry a squaw. I didn't believe it. Even if she didn't act like one, September was an Indian. So what? She didn't make me any more natural. It's true that one night I looked up into the stars and saw her face up there, but if you call that communing there's something wrong with you.

As I drove closer to the Stronghold the road returned to asphalt. I was in a steep ravine, its bottom shaded by giant oaks and its slopes decked with pinyons and junipers. A wooden sign announced that I had arrived.

For such a sacred place it looked a lot like a campground. There was a flat camp area with concrete outhouses and paved walkways and a cement curb. A camp trailer rested on cinder blocks, its awning spread over picnic chairs. I didn't see any people.

I parked at the historical trail and weaved through the pines on a paved footpath. I read the handsomely lettered informational signs.

After all of Thomas Jeffords's good work, the peace he brought was the ruin of the Chiricahua Apache. Cochise's people gave up their hunting grounds for a reservation of rocky farmland and pasture. The warriors went soft. Even with Jeffords as their agent at the Bureau of Indian Affairs, supplies and food promised to the Indians by the government were late or little or none.

Cochise died and his body was entombed somewhere in the inner stronghold. It has never been found.

The United States broke its treaty and herded the Chiricahua off their reservation.

Thomas Jeffords quit his government job and snuck into the desert.

Tuffy followed me through the campground and onto the hiking trail. You could follow the arroyo five miles to a pass then drop into the inner Stronghold. This was where Cochise and his men defended themselves from the white men. On the steep walls behind boulders and buttresses they were invisible to the invaders down in the canyon bottom. This was where Cochise was entombed.

I kicked up dust in the ditch. It felt good. Just as I was starting to warm up, the sun dropped behind a cliff wall and the canyon chilled. I hadn't eaten anything. My knees were starting to wobble. I wasn't going to make it to the inner Stronghold. I stopped there to turn around. It was quiet.

I was alone in the desert. I had come on a journey. Right

then would have been a good time to meet the ghost of Cochise. If I was really part Apache, now I would find out.

So I sat down and tried to be spiritual. I crossed my legs. I concentrated hard to see if I could commune with something. I looked at the sky and the cliffs and the trees. Tuffy cocked her head and watched me with her big black eyes. I didn't know what else to do. I uncrossed my legs. Still nothing happened. Then I saw the campground hosts.

"Would you look at that funny dog!" said the man.

"He's four different colors," said the wife.

They both wore government green vests and caps with official insignias. Here were two very old, very nice white people living in a mobile home in the heart of the Chiricahua homeland. They shook my hand and petted my dog.

"We had three kids, a hundred dogs, and twenty horses," bragged the woman.

She rolled up her checkered sleeves and rubbed Tuffy's belly while her husband recounted a lifetime of breeding show dogs.

"We never had to tell the kids about the birds and the bees," he said. "They were there for the births and the breeding."

"Harold, you remember we took the boys to the 4H show."

Harold clutched my shoulder, either for emphasis or for balance. This was his home. These were my people.

"They had a pig as big as you, just squeezing 'em out."

He stuck out his tongue and demonstrated the noise of piglet birth.

Plop plop plop was the sound he made.

Drops of spittle hit his chin.

Plop plop plop.

CHAPTER 16

The Pigfarm

MOAB, UTAH

A lot of people mistake the desert for nowhere. It's big and stark and nobody demands anything from you or asks any questions or expects you to take part in anything you don't want to. There's no pressure.

That's why so many people trying to get away from everywhere end up in Moab. It feels a lot like nowhere at first. You're surrounded by rock and the next town is fifty miles away. From the banks of the river rises a yellow-brown mountain of uranium tailings. No one can decide what to do with it or how hazardous it is, so it just sits there, radiating.

Of course most people are disappointed by Moab. They imagine the desert will be different and empty but as soon as they get all the way out here the first thing they see is Wendy's and Circle K and Best Western just like wherever they came from. And instead of everyone sitting around weaving and meditating and being spiritual, most of them have to get some dumb job in the summer and go on unemployment in the winter.

But I liked Moab as it was. It would be my home now. I found a campsite above the dump on top of the sandstone fins that enclose the town. It was a good dump. After the mining bust, when citizens were trying to drum up tourism, they had renamed it America's Most Scenic Dump. They rallied a national dump pageant with parades and a Miss Scenic Dump. In the end Moab lost its own contest to a dump somewhere in Alaska, but the dump was still a good place to live while I looked for a house to rent. I got hired by the county to maintain the recreation area just up from the dump on Sand Flats Road. I got Utah license plates for the station wagon and a Utah driver's license with a picture of a beehive on it. None of this would impress September, but I didn't know what else to do.

She was living with Beach Philips now. I didn't know what they did together but now that I was back I wanted them to stop it right away. I drove out to see her, out Spanish Valley to Ken's Lake where they had his school bus parked, but when I got there she wasn't home. Beach invited me in. He told me he'd been working on the bus all winter and wanted to show me around. He'd installed two fifty-gallon water tanks under the bed and an electric pump for the sink. He seemed to be gloating. I took a good look down the shaft of the bus's interior. September's watercolor paintings were taped to the window. There was a propane oven and heater, plus an electric refrigerator, stereo and television.

There was only one bed.

Beach took me outside and showed me the solar panels on the roof that charged the half dozen car batteries stored in the side hatches. He told me he could run all his appliances twenty-four/seven and he'd never run out of juice, not unless there was some major fucking shift in the North American climate. All he needed now was a motorcycle rack and then he'd be totally mobile and self-contained in case the shit went down and he had to duck out from the Man.

We went inside and I sat on the couch. Her sandals were on the floor. Beach said that he and September had used his climbing ropes to steal a dozen power lamps off the ceiling of a warehouse in Junction and were growing a crop in the basement he had told me about. I had the feeling he liked to say her name in front of me. He said she was over at the basement right now, and he would tell me where it was but in his business someone was always trying to rip someone off, and the less people knew about his operation the better.

"You're right," I said. "It's not like I'd want to go out there anyway."

"It's for your own good," he said.

"Does this couch fold out?"

"We're partners now," he said. "She and me. It's just a couch, not a fold-a-bed."

"It's long," I said. "I bet you could sleep on it."

"That thing's the cat's ass," he said and kicked the couch. "It's like a torture chamber. Who'd ever want to sleep on it?"

I leaned back and put my head on the hard wood armrest. The couch sagged in the middle. It hurt just to lay there.

"It's not so bad," I said. "It's pretty all right."

P. D. McCafferty's pigfarm on Murphy Lane was up for rent. It was point nine acres altogether and set back from the road on a long dirt driveway. Pack Creek ran from Spanish Valley down a ditch between the house and the pigpens.

Pud McCafferty walked me and Tuffy across the creek on the bridge made of old doors and railroad ties. He told me he'd been in California the last four years while his daughter had been living here. Now he had to throw her out because it was getting trashed. We looked at the cracked posts and warped plywood where the pigs used to live. They were all gone now. Weeds sprouted up through a heap of tin cans. It was spring and the sugary smell of Russian olives was everywhere.

"I had a stud pig called Sonny," said Pud. "And about fifty sows. That old pig sure loved to fuck."

We kicked through the chit grass to Sonny's stall. It was bigger than the rest.

"This was all tamarack when I moved in," he said. "Me and my wife at the time hacked it all away. I used the trunks for fencepost."

"Is this where you killed them?" I said. "The pigs."

"Until the neighbors filed a complaint," he said. "I don't know if you've ever heard a pig get its throat cut, but it sounds like a rape. So then I trucked them up to slaughter in Price."

We crossed back over the bridge and past the eighteen-wheeler and a pile of motorcycle skeletons. Pud said he didn't like any of the neighbors and pointed to a red cottage by the road. Miss Shanoway was a cunt in particular.

"When I first bought the place I was driving truck."

He said he'd wanted to start a shop to work on semis, but the neighbors wouldn't let him because it was zoned agricultural. So he started raising pigs.

"Fuckum," he said. "They want a farm, they got a farm."

We walked through the shade of a big cottonwood to a long

row of junk cars and a tower of old tires. Pud tapped the hood of
an old pickup and told me it was called Big Blue. That was
another thing. All these cars were his. If anyone came over and
wanted to take parts off them, tell them no, even if they said
they were his friends.

"They have to call me. I don't want them fucking with these
cars."

The retaining walls along the creek were made of appliances.
Washers, dryers, stoves, refrigerators. Pud had bought the place
from an old Nazi who'd escaped from Germany after the war. Just
a little guy, but ripped with muscles. He was a fighter pilot in the
Luftwaffe, had a big fucking eagle tattooed all the way across his
chest with a swastika and a couple Iron Crosses. He was wanted
by the United Nations or something. That old guy rerouted the
goddamn creek with a bulldozer then built these retaining walls
in case it flooded. He just filled these old fridges with dirt and
picked them up with a front loader and stacked them on top of
each other. Held them in place with aircraft cable.

Pud showed me where an entire car was propped on its side
below us to keep the front yard from sliding into the creek. He
lifted the lid off a manhole and I looked down a steel ladder that
led into the car. An old mattress collected twigs and dust. When
it was hot that Nazi would hang out in the car down there.

"Real weird dude," said Pud. There was also an underground
bunker in case of nuclear war. Pud said he found one room when
he was planting the horseshoe stakes. He filled it in with dirt but
there might be more. The neighbors thought there was a net-
work down there, he said. Like in James Bond or something.

The lawn was dead grass and burrs and goat head thorns.

Tuffy rolled around in the dirt. There were three refrigerators. This was Pud McCafferty's home.

"Let me show you the jerky smoker," he said.

He opened up a fridge and a clump of brown leaves dropped onto the dirt.

"Damn, it's been a while."

He swept some more leaves off the rack and showed me where I could put the strips of beef. There was a hibachi at the bottom of the fridge.

"Just burn some oak in there and close it up for a few days. Oak or cherry. Cherry's the best."

Pud kicked the horseshoe stake.

"That's a Chevy axle buried in a half yard of concrete. Feel it."

I grabbed the thing and shook it.

"Solid," I said.

"Damn solid."

Pud looked around and was quiet for a while. Everything in sight was broken. I could hear birds chirping down along the creek.

"I had some good times here," he said. "It could still be nice."

The rent was cheap, so I couldn't say no. Each month I'd pay $100 cash and do $250 of work. I'd bill him five dollars an hour to plaster, patch, paint, clean, weed, plumb, wire, and build. It was a bargain.

I didn't know how to do all the things I said I could, so I asked Beach Philips to come down and give me some advice. He could do anything. If something didn't work he could tell you what you'd done wrong and show you how to fix it.

"Ghetto," was the first word Beach said when he saw my house. "Looks like a bunker."

The Nazi had built it long and low into a hillside. Inside, we looked through the holes in the plaster wall and could see the dirt hillside held back by a wall of tires, each filled solid with dried mud. There were some appliances in there too.

We went into the bathroom. The wall above the tub had been torn out and a sheet of plywood nailed in its place. Behind the plywood the water heater was wedged into the hillside between the tires and draped in slimy fiberglass foam. The toilet didn't flush and sat in a puddle on the linoleum. Beach and I peeked under the mildewed plywood floor. There were no floorboards. Just dirt.

"Way ghetto," said Beach.

All the doors in the house had been kicked in and the jambs splintered. The windows were boarded up. Pud's daughter had lived there with her kid and her boyfriend and they'd broken the windows and punched holes in the wall. Pud told me that it wasn't his daughter who trashed the place but her tweeker friends. When he threw her out she left behind toothbrushes and diapers, a closet full of clothes and sour milk in the refrigerator.

Beach Philips and I stepped into a filthy smelly room that Pud had called the solarium and said he'd built himself. I would have liked to close that room off and forget about it, but there was no door, just a curtain tacked to the door frame. The carpet was always wet and from the middle of it rose a mountain of junk that according to Pud belonged to his best friend Lincoln, who was to get it out of here any day now. The solarium had a high ceiling and a ten-by-ten window that the daughter's tweeker friends had broken. I showed Beach where they'd sealed the crack with silver tape.

"That's a three-hundred-dollar piece of glass," I said. I thought it was an impressive price.

"Smells like shit in here," Beach said.

"Pud put that window in at a special angle to get the most sun in the winter," I said. "He got all the measurements out of the almanac."

"Wonder why he didn't just learn to install it right."

"Oh look. Some cat shit. Tuffy, get away from that."

It was on the carpet where the pipes poked up from the floor. There used to be a sink in the solarium, but Pud's daughter pawned it.

"What this place needs is a match," said Beach, opening up the circuit box. "I can't believe it hasn't burned down already."

Beach rifled through a box of record albums. There were broken lamps and telephone cords and plastic sacks stuffed with clothes. Speaker cabinets balanced on part of a waterbed frame. Then Beach found Pud's welders, a gas welder and an arc welder.

"Bitchen," he said. "I'm gonna need these for my rack."

"He told me not to let anyone take the welders," I said. "They're worth a lot."

"I'm just gonna use them," he said. "Not take them."

Beach asked what kind of tools I had and I showed him my hammers, wrenches, paintbrushes, tool belt, and drywall knives. He picked up the hammer and twirled it like a pistol.

"I had one like this in high school."

We went outside to the picnic table and Beach showed me the Harbor Freight catalog that he carried with him. I popped open two cans of beer and we sat in the sun and looked at the pictures. Beach Philips was serious about tools. He showed me which Sawzall he wanted and told how the Delta compound miter was burlier than the DeWalt. As far as drills, he said, the Milwaukee ain't much, even though a lot of guys still have them. They just like it because it's so heavy they think it's good. Whatever. Makitas are schwag. The Freud is a good drill but it's German and expensive and in terms of a good all-around cordless for the money the DeWalt is your best bet. You probably won't need a hammer drill for what you're doing and if you ever need a Sawzall you can borrow mine when I get it. Don't even look at those Black & Deckers, those are for old men on the weekend. Nobody actually works with a Black & Decker. In the way of circular saws don't waste your money on a fifty-dollar Skilsaw, spend the money on a Porter Cable. That's what everyone has. You can get the framer's saw with the blade on the left and you can see what you're doing as long as you don't cut off your thumb. Speaking of that, check out the new DeWalt with the electric brake. It's an extra sixty bucks but it might save you a finger some day.

I ordered the DeWalt twelve-volt drill and a set of bits, a fifty-foot heavy gauge extension cord, and the cheap Skilsaw because it was all I could afford.

My first job at the pigfarm was taping and painting the bedroom ceiling. It was cracked and greasy, mostly white with a corner of beige roller strokes where some painter had started then quit. Up on the ladder I thought how good the ceiling would look from down there on the bed with September.

I heard the dirtbike buzz down the driveway and I went outside. Beach was driving and September was on the back with her arms and legs wrapped around him. It was the first time I had seen them together like that. I didn't like it.

"Isn't this place a shithole?" Beach said to September as soon as he got off the bike. He said it loud enough for me to hear. "It's like a compound."

September stood there and kicked the dirt with a straight leg. Tuffy came out from the house and trotted about and September petted her and I stood there not saying anything.

"You got a dog," she said. "Good for you."

Tuffy started to nip Beach's heels and he gave her a soft kick in the mouth.

"Don't be a jerk," said September.

"That's how you train a dog," he said. "Just ask anyone."

"I don't want to ask anyone."

"I'm just telling you how it is."

"I'm just telling you don't be a jerk."

While September played with Tuffy, Beach and I hauled the arc welder out of the solarium and onto the bed of the eighteen-wheeler and laid out the steel tubing we'd bought the day before. He said the semi was a good place to work because it was grounded.

"You just want a reason to hang out on it and look like a badass," September said. She threw her leg over the motorcycle and sat on it with her toes dangling above the ground. She said she had some errands to do and would be back in a while.

"What do you mean errands?" said Beach.

"Just stuff."

"When will you be back?"

September rolled her eyes and smiled just barely and threw up her hands. Then without answering the question she kicked the starter and zoomed up the driveway in a plume of dust.

Oh, I thought. A girl on a motorcycle.

Once Beach got into his army jacket and welder's helmet I knew it would be a good chance to see her alone. I told him I had to go out for some drywall tape and drove off. I bumped along the dirt roads behind Ken's Lake. The school bus wasn't there. The rangers made them move every fourteen days. I back-tracked along Spanish Valley Drive to Johnson's Up-on-Top and found the bus tucked behind two pinyons with the Enduro rested on its kickstand out front. I knocked and went in. September was sitting on the couch painting with watercolors. The bed was made up. Everything was in order. She looked up and then looked back down like she wasn't surprised to see me.

"Where do you sleep?" I said.

She went on painting her stupid painting. I stomped down the stairs and walked around the desert and picked up rocks and threw them. Everything was fine. I threw some more rocks. I was an adult. After a while she came out and found me. She held my hand between hers.

"I missed you," she said.

"What happened to your teeth?"

"Did you miss me?"

"They look different," I said. "Did you get something done to them?"

"You're the one with the nice teeth."

"You look different now."

"I'm still the same."

"Why don't you tell him to floss?" I said.

"We're splitting the money fifty-fifty," she said. "Pretty soon I'll have a lot of it."

"There's all disgusting yellow gunk in his teeth."

"Don't you still want to go to Spain with me?"

"No."

"Yes you do."

"Okay, I do."

"Now go home and be friends with him," she said. "You can't come over here or you'll ruin everything."

When I got back to the pigfarm Beach was still welding and a package from Harbor Freight sat on the porch. I tore open the box and grabbed the saw and Beach hopped down off the flatbed and we went straight for the wood heap and took turns cutting up logs and old boards and scraps of particle board. We cut up an old plywood sign and a broken chest of drawers. The Skilsaw screamed and the sawdust flew. We cut up a broom-stick. Once we'd cut everything into small pieces we picked up the small pieces and cut them into tiny pieces. After half an hour the Skilsaw made a pop and a groan and stopped.

"See how yaur," said Beach. "Shoulda got the Porter Cable."

I put it back in the box and the next day sent it off with a check for the left-blade Porter Cable framer's saw.

The Spanish Valley water main erupted. There was a small flood out by the golf course and a lot of people lost service for a day. Too much pressure in the Valley, said Beach Philips. He was working overtime driving a backhoe for the repair crew so he had to put off welding the motorcycle rack. He didn't have time to come over to the compound. That's what he called the pigfarm now.

I was working too. I worked Wednesdays through Sundays up on the Sand Flats. I carried a walkie-talkie and told people where they could and couldn't camp and I dug postholes and planted cedar fence around the parking areas. The job was good for the Earth but what I liked best was getting to drive a little green six-wheeler fast on dirt roads.

I was also busy at the pigfarm. I cut the water heater out from behind the shower and installed it in the laundry room. I hung a sheet of Masonite and replumbed the shower. I fixed the toilet. I drywalled the breakfast nook and painted the kitchen. It was good to get things in order.

The first time I ran the washing machine I heard a gurgling sound in the solarium. Murky washwater erupted out of the drain pipe like a little geyser. The piles of cat shit floated in a puddle. I glued a PVC cap on the pipe and turned the machine back on. Then the washwater bubbled out in the yard and flushed into the creek. Tuffy sniffed at the murky water and turned up her nose. I reached down to see where it was coming from and cut my finger on something.

While I was standing there squeezing my finger an El Camino sputtered down the driveway with its muffler dragging in the dirt. The man who got out looked like an old bear in the zoo.

"I'm Link," he shouted. "I come to get my things."

Tuffy ran past me and lay on her back at his feet, and he bent over to rub her belly. He reached over to shake but I held up my finger and showed him it was bleeding.

"Can't believe Pud found someone to take this place on," he said. "When I lived here I had a job at the dump and get this, lots of times I'd wake up at night and look out the window and think I was still at work."

Lincoln laughed and his belly jiggled through his shirt. He ran his fingers through his beard, plucked an unlit cigarette from behind his ear, sucked it, then put it back. In a very short time I knew a whole lot about him. He told me he used to drive the frontloader at the dump, the scenic dump, and he could drive equipment like a son of a bitch. But then he'd been fired from his job at the dump for, get this, he said, insubordination. Insubordination at the dump. They wanted him to bury all that perfectly good lumber, all that furniture, all those appliances that could still be fixed, and he said fuck it, so they fired him.

When I pulled back the curtain to the solarium and Lincoln saw his heap of belongings, he stopped short. He mouthed the cigarette. It was limp and dirty. After a while he ran his fingers over the stereo cabinet.

"What the fuck am I gonna do with this shit?" he said. He blew a cloud of dust off the record stack. He stood there. It's hard to see everything you have thrown in a big pile.

"Stinks in here," he said.

He said that one of these days he'd come back and haul everything away but right now money was tight and he was staying with his old lady in Thompson and there wasn't any room. I told him I could drag it all onto the lawn so he could pick it up easier and he said he'd appreciate that. As soon as he drove off I started hauling the mountain of broken furniture and rusted tools and musty clothing into the dirt outside.

It was good to do some work around the house. The sun was

up. Tuffy nipped my cuffs and I gave her a little kick. It was good to have a dog well trained. It was good to get some work done and to get things in order. That's what was really needed, not to go run off to the desert, but to get things in order. Soon the pile of junk was complete and it sat in the lawn.

Then it rained. Storm clouds rolled down the mountains and black drops thumped down in the dirt. The sky flashed. The rain fell hard. Lincoln's velvet armchair turned the color of wine and water dripped down the side of the waterbed. From inside I watched the water run off the lawn and puddle at the front door.

The rain drummed on the roof and thunder boomed. Then rainwater came dripping through the ceiling. I set paint buckets and kitchen pots in the entryway and watched them fill up. Once they were full I dumped them down the sink then set them down to fill again.

It stormed most of the week. When it was over Lincoln's stuff was saturated and a small lake covered the driveway. I figured it was from the rain but after a few days of sun the heap was dry but the lake was still there, and one morning I saw water spurting out from the hillside along the driveway.

The watermain running from the street to my house had broken. I called Pud in California and told him there was too much pressure in the Valley. He explained how to dig it up and patch it and said he would come out in the summer and lay a new one with a DitchWitch. And he'd put on a new roof too.

Beach had a day off and came over to weld. When he got there I'd already dug into the soft moist berm and found the pipe. He showed me how to cut the blown section with a hacksaw and splice in a replacement, and when I was done I left him there to weld and I hurried to work.

I still made it on time. I was supposed to be building a fence but I was already sick of digging so I just leaned on my shovel in the sunlight. We were out on a dirt road where no one could see us anyway. When summer got here I was going to go back to my job on the river, but on days like this I didn't mind the county job at all. I was working out in the desert with the snowy mountains above and I was allowed to bring Tuffy and she could run around all day long.

The guy I was working with leaned on his shovel and rolled a cigarette. He said that if we heard the supervisors coming all we had to do was point our fingers across the way and they'd think we were talking about something important or making a decision. He'd done this kind of work all his life.

Then a motor came buzzing up the road. But instead of the supervisor it was Beach Philips on his dirtbike.

"Get home quick," he said. "Link's ripping the place off."

By the time I got there, Lincoln had already loaded a flatbed with furniture and now he and another guy were loading the welders into the back of the El Camino. A third guy was tinkering under the hood of the semi with a pair of jumper cables.

"Those are Pud's welders," I said.

"He said it was all right," said Lincoln. "Do you have the keys to the semi?"

I told him I didn't. I went inside and looked around. I didn't notice anything of mine missing. Lincoln and his friends packed up and left.

"Ghetto," Beach said. "I wasn't done with that arc welder."

September wasn't allowed to drive. Her VW Bug was parked outside her mom's house and as part of her probation she wasn't allowed to drive it. It was a pain for her because just when her probation for shoplifting had ended, now she was back on for not paying speeding tickets. A sheriff's deputy drove by the house each night to make sure the car was still there.

Beach Philips asked me if he could borrow my car on his day off to go to Grand Junction to get some supplies. He made it clear that September was going with him. He didn't ask me to come along. I said all right.

When the day came and they showed up, Beach said he'd been called into work and couldn't go to Junction. But the trip couldn't wait. He asked if I'd let September take my car by herself. I looked over at her. She was petting the dog and wouldn't look up. He said she knew all about the hoses and valves and special lightbulbs that they needed.

"Whatever he says," said September. He handed her a roll of cash and she tucked it in her sock. I didn't like the way she just took that money from him like it was an everyday thing.

As soon as Beach rode off she gave the finger his way.

"You're coming with me," she said. "Promise not to tell Beach."

We drove the station wagon up the river road past Hittle Bottom and into the Cisco desert. It was May and the wind was blowing.

"How much money did he give you?" I said.

September pressed her socks against the windshield and

squirmed and sucked her finger. Then she lay on her back and dropped her head in my lap.

"Dude, you were right about the floss. He needs to go to the dentist or something."

"Does he pay for everything?"

"Let me see your teeth."

"I'm trying to drive."

"Open up."

"There."

"Those are nice teeth," she said. "Maybe you two could trade."

"I don't want his teeth."

"I don't keep track of who pays for what to answer your question."

"I don't want anything he has."

"You can't have it," she said. "Not right now anyway."

I kept driving through Cisco town and onto the Interstate. She lay in my lap with her eyes closed. I tried to think of something to say to remind her how much she used to like me.

"Do you still have that painting?" I said.

"Which one?"

"Now that I have a house I could hang it up."

September bit my shirt and made a growling noise.

"I burned it."

"Before, I didn't have a place for it," I said.

"I had a bunch of stuff I didn't want to carry around so I took it all out in my mom's yard and burned it. She thought it was funny."

We sped over the shallow forks of the Colorado and got off

the highway and drove to the hardware store. By then I needed to get out of the car. My knees were wobbly, and walking across the parking lot I felt like I'd just got off a ship.

Beach was right that September knew a lot about PVC pipe and fixtures and fittings and garden fertilizers. The guy in the garden department thought she was a real pro. She bought five of the fittings and when we got to the car she had twenty more in her pockets.

In the Salvation Army I asked the clerk if we could get the bag-sale price even though the sale didn't start until the next day.

"My husband and I are only in town for today," said September. "I had to pick him up from jail."

"I see," said the clerk. "I suppose that would be fine, the sale price."

We filled a brown bag with a down parka, four shirts and a pair of jeans for three dollars. I tried to put in a two-dollar dress for September but she stole it instead.

By then it was afternoon and we were hungry. We drove to Pancho Villa and parked across the street. September darted in front of an eighteen-wheeler then laughed at me from the opposite curb while I waited for the green light.

"You're cute when you're a chicken," she said.

We got a big smooth booth beneath a mural of Mexican landscape and ate chile rellenos and drank margaritas. September told me she'd never been served in a bar. She lifted her sock feet under the table and set them in my lap.

"This is what Spain will be like," I said.

She smiled and sucked on the straw.

"Don't be such a dork, dude."

CHAPTER 17

A Glock for September

MOAB, UTAH

You can never be nowhere. No matter how hard you try. Not even in the middle of the desert. The further you get from one place the closer you are to someplace else, and when you try to drop out of the world altogether you'll find that wherever you land is still a part of it. There will be people there who make things just as complicated as the things you were trying to get away from.

So you may as well settle on a place and get it in order. In the backyard of the Moab Building Center was a stack of custom windows that contractors had never picked up. I found a fancy double-paned slider that was just a bit too short and a bit too wide for the bedroom and I bought it for sixty dollars. I tore out the old window frame and built up the sill with junk lumber. The new window fit fine. I lifted the bedroom door off the jamb and drove it into C & R Glass for a forty-dollar custom pane. But even with the new windows the bedroom was like a cave and I needed to turn on the lights in the daytime.

At night it was lonely on the pigfarm and sometimes I

wished I had a TV or something. I thought of teaching Tuffy a trick but there was nothing really I wanted her to do. I showed her how to balance a pencil on her nose. She was big enough to jump up on the bed with me, and we lay there trying to sleep.

It was getting hot again. Since Link had taken all the window screens the moths and mayflies and mosquitoes swarmed the reading lamp. The ceiling looked like germs through a microscope. When the bugs buzzed into my nose I turned off the light and lay there awake and listened to the creek and crickets and the hum of the refrigerator. I could smell a skunk. I got up and walked up the dirt driveway in the moonlight. Water from the main bubbled out of the hillside into a glassy pond.

In the morning I was outside digging it up when Beach Philips and September came down the driveway on the Enduro. September smiled at me from behind him so that he couldn't see it. He didn't know about our trip to Grand Junction.

"If I was you I'd get a backhoe and dig a new watermain," said Beach. "Right there under the driveway."

"I can't drive a backhoe."

"I can."

It was in the nineties for the first time that year. We went inside and switched on the swamp cooler. With the watermain shot, it just blew in hot air.

Beach and September were on their way to buy her a handgun. Beach said that Mad Albert the drunk had come by while September was out sunbathing.

"I wasn't sunbathing, dumbass. I was lying out."

"She was naked."

"Let me tell it," said September. "I had to lock myself in his stupid bus for three hours with a butcher knife and some weirdo outside the door."

Beach already had some rifles and a revolver but he said they needed a semiautomatic pistol. He explained what automatic and caliber meant and the difference between a .44 and a .357 Magnum and a nine-mil. He said the gun September wanted was a Beretta nine-millimeter semiautomatic with a fifteen-round clip. But now with the Brady Bill you could only get a ten-round clip.

"We really need a fifteen-round clip."

"What's wrong with ten rounds?" I said. I didn't like the way he said we.

"What if the guy shooting at you has fifteen?"

Beach said his friend Schroeder had a fifteen-round Beretta he wanted to sell. I had seen Schroeder hiking up Mill Creek before with a pistol in a holster and a Bowie knife strapped to his thigh and I asked him why all the weapons and he said in case he saw a cougar. Now Schroeder wanted a lighter gun for backpacking. He liked the plastic Glock 40-caliber at Brigg's Outdoor and Hardware. September would buy the Glock then trade it to Schroeder for the Beretta. But to buy the Glock you needed a Utah driver's license. September's was revoked and Beach's was from Idaho because up there the Man couldn't track you as well.

"Since you have a license," he said, "you could buy the Glock and sell it to Schroeder."

Beach told me it was very legal and a part of the right to bear arms. I didn't have anything else to do so I said if he'd help me dig then I'd do it.

Once the pipe was patched the three of us drove in my station wagon down to Brigg's Outdoor. I pointed at the 40-cal through the glass and the girl handed it to me. It was cold in my hand and heavy. The way the girl behind the counter watched me I was pretty sure I wasn't holding it right. Beach snatched it out of my hand and made some quick click-clack noises then gave it back.

"So this is the one you want?" he said like he was my dad and it was a baseball mitt.

"You bet." I handed the gun to the girl. "I'll take this one."

She called over the manager and they asked to see my license and call my name into the police computer and roll my finger-prints. We went outside to wait for the security check to clear. September handed me a roll of twenties thicker than her wrist.

"Six-forty should be enough," she said.

"So now it's registered in my name," I said to Beach. "What happens when I sell it?"

"It's still in your name."

"For how long?"

"As long as they keep records."

"So if someone kills someone with it the police will arrest me?"

"They might come looking for you," he said. "That's why you get a receipt when you sell it. Hold on to that receipt for the rest of your life in case there's trouble. But Schroeder isn't gonna kill anyone. He just likes guns to play with."

We got the Glock and drove over to Schroeder's bus which was parked down the river at the culvert before the potash mine. We climbed inside. Schroeder lifted the Beretta out of a padded ammo can and took out the clip to show it was unloaded, then opened the chamber and held it up so that me and Beach and September could all see for ourselves that it was empty. Beach did the same with the Glock. Schroeder was very competent at counting money and writing gun receipts. I trusted him. It was no big deal.

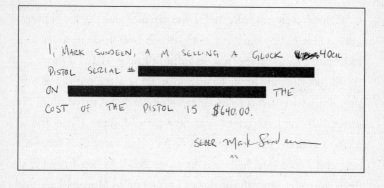

I, MARK SUNDEEN, A M SELLING A GLOCK ▓▓40cal
PISTOL SERIAL # ██████████████████████
ON ████████████████████ THE
COST OF THE PISTOL IS $640.00.

SELLER Mark Sundeen

We left Schroeder's bus and at the pawnshop bought a 100 bullets for the firearm. Beach had started calling it that. We drove up Sand Flats Road to the old target range behind the dump and it was sunny on the mesa below the snowy mountains. We slipped under a fence and Beach Philips loaded the cartridge and rammed it into the firearm with the heel of his hand.

"You go first," he said and handed it to September. "It's yours anyway."

September held up the gun and without aiming squeezed off fifteen shots at the old TVs and water heaters. Beach reloaded it and handed it to me. It was pretty hard to hit anything the way it bucked and I just held it at my hip and pumped bullets into the hillside. We shot everything up pretty quick then went back and bought the rest of the ammo at the pawnshop and fired that too. Some hunters drove up with their rifles but after watching us for a while backed onto the blacktop and drove away. I said motherfucker and kept shooting.

Things were complicated. I was tired of waiting for September to finish her business with Beach and I thought that if something didn't happen soon I didn't know what I'd do.

When the pipe broke again and water spurted out of the hillside, I just went to the road and wrenched the valve shut. My water bill for last month was fifty-three dollars. I had leaked 12,500 gallons. Pud told me to deduct the water bills from the rent and I told him he better fix it for good. When I needed to flush the toilet or wash the dishes I hiked up to Murphy Lane and opened the valve, and by the time I was through with the water there was a puddle in the driveway. There was still too much pressure in the pipes and I didn't know what to do about it.

A few days after it broke I dug up the main and replaced the cracked section. Then I walked around the farm with my dog and inspected the junk cars and crossed the bridge and laid my hand on the pig stall. I put away the shovel. June was almost here, river season was about to begin, and I'd given notice to my boss at the county. Everything was in order. Then September's Beetle Bug skidded down the drive.

"I thought you weren't allowed to drive that thing," I said.

"Well we better not get caught then," she said. "Get in."

She rolled through the stop sign at Mill Creek Drive and sped out of town to the river road. She went a bit too fast for my liking but it was good to be with her, and I held on to the little handle and tried not to look over at her.

"Beach says I'm not allowed to talk to you."

"You're tailgating."

"It takes some nerve to tell someone that."

"Well you are. You're about to rear-end him."

"Not what you said. What Beach said."

"It's no wonder you lost your license."

"So I promised him, swore to him, that I wouldn't see you at all."

She drove up into Castle Valley to a small house where nobody lived, then unlocked a padlock and we climbed down into a cellar.

It was cool and lush down there. The plants stood in rows and columns on a plywood platform and grew together in a big jungly thicket that crowded the lights on the ceiling. The smell was enough to knock you out. September snipped a branch and held it toward me.

"No one was supposed to see this," I said.

"Mmm, smell," she said. "Harvest."

"Put that thing down."

"I do all the work here," she said. "Then Beach tells me how I should have done it different."

"There's a light burned out."

"What's to stop me from taking it all?" she said. "I grew it."

"Do you have a spare bulb?"

"Hey, wanna hear something funny?" She unscrewed the old bulb and put in the new one. "Guess what Beach's real name is."

"Let's go somewhere."

"He told me I couldn't tell anyone."

"Okay, what is it?"

"You have to guess."

"I give up."

"Brigham," she said. "Isn't that the best?"

"No way."

"Go look at his license, dude. But you didn't hear it from me."

We drove back to town, but instead of taking me home to the compound she gunned it up past the dump to where the road turned to dirt. I held on and braced with my feet. We rattled past the pinyons and slick rock domes, up through the squeeze in the road and out onto the mesa. The snowpeaks in front of us were pink in the sunset. White clouds clung to Haystack Mountain.

"The thing I like about you," said September, "is that you never tell me what to do."

She punched it. We launched off the bumps in the road and laughed at the crack and scrape of metal against rock. In a flat bare spot where people usually camped she said watch this dude, donuts, and she spun the Bug in tight circles until it broached on a sage brush and she yelled and laughed and told me to get out and push.

September drove me to the head of my driveway. Before I got out she kissed me on the cheek.

"You look pale," she said.

"I'm carsick."

She said she had some things to do. Tuffy ran up and rolled in the dirt, and September took off with a screech. I walked carefully down to the house one foot in front of the other.

The driveway was flooded.

Goddamn goddamn goddamn goddamn. The pressure was too much. I cranked down the valve with a wrench and drove out to Johnson's Up-on-Top.

Beach Philips was running his orbital sander off a generator and laying into the front bumper of the bus. The motorcycle rack he'd welded was finished and bolted to the bumper.

"Looks good," I said.

He propped his safety glasses on his forehead and asked if I'd seen September. I said I hadn't. He said they'd been popped by the ranger and had to move in the next day or two. I told him I wasn't going to take any more lines from Pud McCafferty and I'd dig the watermain myself.

"I knew it was coming," he said grinning.

When he finished painting we drove back to the compound. It was hot and it hadn't rained in a month and except for the leak the driveway was dry and dusty. Beach had a 100-foot tape and we measured that the driveway was 210 feet. It was the only access from road to house, so that's how long the ditch needed to be. Pud's idea had been to replace the pipe in the hillside along the driveway, which with a DitchWitch would only take a couple hours. The only problem was that the hillside was so eroded that we'd have to lay the pipe farther back, on the neighbor's property. This was a situation for Beach Philips and me. It meant that one of us would have to go next door and ask permission to dig a 200-foot ditch in their yard.

"Fuck Pud," said Beach. "DitchWitches are for pussies."

The hillside would just keep eroding, he said, and once the pipe was exposed to sun it would burst again. If we wanted to solve this pressure problem for good we needed to bury the main under the driveway, not next to it. And if it was under the driveway it needed to be at least seven feet down or else the weight of the cars would push down the frost and freeze the pipes. Couldn't hurt to go eight feet just to be safe. A DitchWitch only went four feet deep. Beach Philips kicked the dirt.

"We're gonna need a backhoe on this one."

At the lumberyard we bought eleven lengths of PVC plus the joiners, primer, and cement. We reserved the backhoe for Saturday from G&C Rentals. Beach said Saturday was the best because if no one reserved it for Sunday, which they never do, then you could keep it till first thing Monday morning. That was good timing for Beach. By Monday September would have the harvesting done and they'd be ready to weigh and pack and sell.

Since Beach needed a place to move his bus, I told him he could bring it down to the compound. He pulled down the driveway Friday afternoon, the Enduro on the rack and September tailing him in the Bug. A cloud of dust followed them into the yard and they parked by the scrapped motorbikes under the cottonwood.

September and I dropped Beach at G&C and he headed back to the pigfarm in the backhoe. He didn't like us driving off together. At City Market she stole pasta and ice cream and fresh bread from the bakery. I bought a twelvepack of three-two beer.

"Dude," she said when we got in my station wagon. We sat there in the hot parking lot. "Why don't you ever do anything wrong?"

"I'm no good at it."

"You could learn. Look at me. I keep getting better."

I turned the key and the motor started.

"Let's not go back yet," she said. "We could sit here a while."

"The ice cream will melt."

"I don't want to go back there yet."

I turned off the car. The wind blew a funnel of dust across the parked cars. Some people rode by on bikes.

"What if I asked you to do something wrong?" she said. "Would that make it easier?"

"I'm going to have a beer if we're just going to sit here."

"Don't you know that if you're just nice to people they take everything?"

"It's a twist-off."

"Maybe for you it's easy to be good but not for me."

I started the car again.

"You didn't answer the question," she said. "Answer the question. Would you do something wrong for me?"

"I'd do it. I'd do anything. How's that?"

"No you wouldn't," she said. "I won't even ask you."

"Look," I said. I slammed the beer bottle down on the carpet next to the emergency brake and it fizzed up and ran down the glass onto my hand. "Not everybody wants to own you."

"Beach does."

"I don't."

"Yes you do."

"Fine," I said. "Maybe. Goddamn it I spilled. So what?"

"That ruins everything."

The engine was running. We drove out Mill Creek Drive and up Murphy Lane. I didn't know what to say. There were no other cars. The road was bumpy. The beer was getting warm.

"Do you know what I'm going to do?" she said.

"I think so."

"Are you going to stop me?"

"No."

Back at home we ate out on the picnic table. Beach Philips and September and me. Even at dusk it was too hot to be inside, but under the big shade tree it was nice. The frogs and cicadas sang from the creek and purple tamarisk feathers floated on the dust. There was red sunlight in the windshield of the semi and in the windows of the school bus and in the boxy glass cockpit of the backhoe. There were no clouds or any signs of the weather going bad and it was fine down on the compound.

At six A.M. I heard the cough and roar of the diesel motor. Beach and September had brewed some tea in the bus and were drinking it while the Cat warmed up. It was 84 degrees.

"Do you have the firearm?" Beach said.

She pulled the Beretta out of the glove box and waved it around. Beach told her not to conceal it in the glove box and that she had to put it on the dashboard or in the trunk, and she just smiled and put it back where she'd found it. Then she pecked each of us on the cheek.

"You boys have fun digging your little ditch."

She peeled up the drive in the dust. Beach climbed up in the cockpit. He drove to the edge of the house and sunk the bucket with a loud creak and dug out a chunk of soil. The arm lurched and straightened and showed clean steel rods under its rusted armor. Black smoke floated out of the exhaust pipe. It was loud. Now I was going to work and not worry about what anyone else was doing.

When the ditch was ten feet long Beach killed the motor and we jumped down in there and snapped off the existing pipe. My job was to follow behind the backhoe at the bottom of the ditch with a flat-blade shovel and build a cradle for the new watermain. Then I'd set down the twenty-foot pipelengths and cement them together.

At lunchtime Beach taught me how to run the backhoe.

"I'm into the philosophy of heavy equipment," he said. "It's a living thing, like a dinosaur or a monster, and you're the brain. It will do anything you tell it to."

I got up there and clunked around. With the hand levers and foot pedals I could move the big bucket back and forth and plunk it down on the dirt. There were always four things to think about at once and it was hot and I was having fun. I pressed with my right foot when I meant to pull with my left hand, and the arm made a wild swing. My section of ditch wasn't as neat and square as Beach's. He decided not to show me how to use the outriggers.

Then the man from G&C Rentals pulled up in a big pickup and told us that someone had just rented the backhoe for tomorrow. The guy would pick it up from us at nine in the morning if that was all right.

Beach said it was ghetto but whatever.

Now we had to hurry. Beach got back in the cockpit and fired up the diesel. The machine heaved and creaked and spit out fumes, the arms and legs flying this way and that. It went faster and faster in a clunky rhythm.

Scoop pivot dump pivot. Scoop pivot dump pivot.

Outriggers up, beep beep beep.

Outriggers down, shovel extends.

Scoop pivot dump pivot. Scoop pivot dump pivot.

I was down in the ditch covered in dirt. The Cat was roaring. It was more fluid now and Beach dug faster and deeper.

The walls were taller than me. I couldn't see anything but sky and steel bucket. When we crossed the gas pipe Beach hollered down at me from the cockpit.

"You gotta dig around it with the shovel or else I'll cut it."

I nodded and stabbed with the shovel. I was tired.

"Careful not to cut the wire."

I kept digging. The diesel churned away.

"There's a wire a few inches above the pipe," he yelled. "Don't cut it."

Just then I saw the wire and swung the blade and watched it slice through the wire. I looked up at Beach and he killed the motor.

"See how yaur!" he said and hopped down from the cockpit. "Go get me a wirestripper."

Beach Philips spliced the wire and got digging again and by dusk the ditch was dug. 210 feet long, eight feet deep, bordered on one side by mountains of fresh red dirt. We set the pipe and cemented it. The faucets worked. All we needed to do in the morning was bury it.

It was dark out and moths danced around the bright kitchen window. Beach and I went inside and ate potatoes and soup. I was aching all over. We didn't talk. The only thing to talk about would have been why September hadn't come home yet. When Tuffy and I lay down in bed we heard him kickstart his dirtbike and buzz over the dunes in the driveway.

It was a hot night and I didn't sleep much. I never heard Beach come home. At first light he fired up the backhoe but didn't come inside to get me. I got dressed and went outside.

He was up in the cockpit and he stared away from me while it warmed up. He hadn't slept. September's car was not up at the head of the driveway or anywhere else. He didn't have to say anything.

She was gone. She had taken it all.

I jumped down in the ditch. I started covering the pipe with a buffer layer of dirt. Beach was up above me with a ton of dirt in the shovel. I backed away from it. The Cat lurched forward and a landslide thundered down in front of me. Then another. He could bury me if he wanted to. I turned around and buried the pipe as fast as I could, the ditch filling in behind me.

Scoop pitch pat, scoop pitch pat, scoop pitch pat.

The dirt was falling behind me.

Scoop pitch pat, scoop pitch pat, scoop pitch pat.

By nine o'clock when the two men arrived to pick up the backhoe, Beach was leveling off the driveway with the shovel. He left it running and one of them climbed in and drove off.

The water main was finished. Beach Philips loaded his dirt-bike onto his bus. He didn't want to talk to me and I didn't want to talk to him. I paid Beach cash for helping me. He started the bus and rumbled up the driveway. I didn't ask where he was going.

Now they were both gone. I sat down at the picnic table. Everything was simple again. I had the place to myself again. It was empty. My dog was asleep in the weeds. It was very quiet and there was nothing to do.

I got in my car and with the wheels spinning in the fresh dirt pulled onto Murphy Lane and drove down to City Market. I was dirty. I pushed a cart up and down the aisles and looked at all the things I didn't want. I couldn't think about anything.

IN THE SEVENTH DISTRICT COURT

In and For Grand County, State of Utah

THE CITY OF MOAB,		
Plaintiff,	)	INFORMATION
VS	)	
	)	NO. 941700115 MC
MARK SUNDEEN,	)	
▓▓▓ North Main	)	
Moab, Utah 84532	)	
DOB: 10/14/70	)	
Defendant.	)	

COMES NOW William L. Benge, Moab City Attorney, and states on information and belief that the Defendant committed in the above named city and county, the crime(s) of:

RETAIL THEFT in violation of Moab City Ordinance #92-06 (76-6-602, UCA), in that the said Defendant, MARK SUNDEEN, on the ▓▓▓▓▓▓▓▓▓▓▓▓▓▓▓▓ A.D., 1994, at approximately 1:00 p.m., at at 425 South Main, Main, Moab, Grand County, State of Utah, did take possession of, conceal, or carry away, transfer or cause to be carried away or transferred, merchandise displayed, held, stored, or offered for sale in a retail mercantile establishment with the intention of retaining such merchandise or with the intention of depriving the merchant permanently of the possession, use or benefit of such merchandise without payment of the retail value of such merchandise, to-wit: (2) breadsticks, having a total value of $.30, a Class B Misdemeanor.

Victim: City Market

DATED this _____ day of _____, A.D., 1994.

William L. Benge,
Moab City Attorney

The walls of food were like a maze I was trapped in and the glaring electric light hurt my eyes and the tinny artificial music would not leave me alone. The people on the cereal boxes were insane.

I went to the bakery and picked an Italian-style breadstick from the bin and took a bite. It was warm and soft and tasted like fake butter and salt. I ate another. Then I left the empty cart and walked to the door.

Excuse me, sir, did you know you just ate two breadsticks?

Yes.

The clerk had nicks on his neck from shaving that morning. I didn't want to be next to him or talk to him.

Were you going to pay for them?

No.

He led me to the small room at the front of the store and after I talked to the associate manager and then the manager a policeman arrived and searched the wastebasket to see I hadn't hidden anything and cuffed my hands behind my back and led me out, and the automatic doors parted for us and we walked together in the hot mean sun to the black-and-white patrol car waiting out front.

CLOSING

CHAPTER 18

Das Marlboro Abenteurer Team

LAKE POWELL, UTAH

I always lit a cigarette above the big rapids. I knew they would like it. Summer had come and I was running rafts for the Marlboro Abenteurer Team. They were German. They had won an action trip to Utah by filling out a form that came in the cigarette pack. If there were any qualifications or requirements, I never learned.

Having adventures was the one thing I was good at. I'd been on plenty of them before. Now I was getting paid for it. It was my job. This one had sponsors and uniforms and photographers. It made it seem more real.

The Abenteurers wore red. They wore red caps and shorts and jumpsuits with the Marlboro logo. They stuffed red Abenteurer sleeping bags into their red Abenteurer backpacks. Across the bow of the rafts, foot-tall letters said Marlboro. We bobbed on the river like cigarette boxes. They gave me a hat and t-shirt so that in the photos I looked like part of the Team. When we paddled down Westwater Canyon on the Colorado we had a j-rig run ahead and wait below each rapid with the cameras.

"Having adventures was one thing I was good at. . . . It was my job."

Hit zee vaves in zee center, cried Fritz. Jurgen and Fritz were the organizers and had bushy walrus mustaches and my boss told me to do whatever they said. They liked the Team members to wear the uniform, perform cheers and calisthenics, and eat sausage sliced from heavy tubes. They had told my boss that I ruined a photo because in my straw hat I looked like a hillbilly fisherman. So after that I wore the Marlboro cap and smoked a lot.

I knew how to act. They liked me for it. When one day the photographer demanded to be tied into a harness on the bow of the boat, I wanted to warn him he would drown if we flipped. But when I saw his glare I just said okay. And I didn't complain when a helicopter buzzed ten feet above my raft with a video camera and blasted my hat off and blew the whitecaps upriver. It was my job.

Fritz and Jurgen thought plain rafting wasn't exciting enough. They wanted the boats to flip. It was June and Westwater Canyon was peaking from the snowmelt. Upstream the campgrounds were underwater. All the rapids but Skull were washed out but the water was fast and scary as it boiled along the rock walls. It was like one big toilet getting flushed. Once you started you couldn't slow down or stop. At Little D Creek my stomach was in a knot. I didn't eat any lunch. Then we untied the boats and launched.

The Germans had told me to eddy out often to give the photographers time to set up below. I tried to pull into a cove above Funnel Falls. The boat hit the wall and folded and started to ride up the rock. Water rushed in from upstream and paddles and arms and legs flailed around. I got a shoe in the face when somebody went overboard. Now we were on an adventure. Finally we spun off the wall. I was still in the boat with water to my waist. The river was churning with paddles and bailbuckets and Abenteurers.

I pulled in two swimmers but a third was way downriver. He went under for a five count, popped up, spit, went under. I chucked my throwbag but missed him by a lot. Then one of the Germans either found another rope or coiled up mine and hit the guy on the ear from about forty feet. We pulled him in right above Skull. Since only two of us still had paddles I told them all to just hold on and high-side. We drifted sideways into the hole. The cameras flashed and Fritz and Jurgen howled. We got pummeled. The boat was so swamped that it stayed upright.

It was a pretty good job. It paid eighty-five dollars a day plus tips and at the end of each adventure was a party at White's Ranch with steak, ribs, and chicken, plus a trough of Budweiser and an athletic German man mixing margaritas. Cowboys yodeled western songs. The Abenteurers danced with whatever women they could find and then with each other. Packs of Marlboros were arranged in neat stacks on all the tables. I filled my pockets.

In midsummer Beach Philips came back to river guiding. He still thought it was beneath him, but he needed the money. There was no backhoe work. It was this or toss pizzas. We were working for the Man.

I thought that he would have been bitter about September but he told me he forgave her. He'd even talked to her on the telephone. Everyone has some bad blood in them, he said. Unlike people in stories who just disappear into the desert and are never seen again, September just drove to Albuquerque. She did not turn into a hawk. And when she met up with the guy who had arranged to buy the harvest, he didn't buy it at all. Instead he kicked her once in the stomach. Then he drove away in the Volkswagen with the goods and the firearm and her sleeping bag and everything else she owned. When she talked to Beach Philips she was trying to get a ride to California. She wanted to get away from everything. I wished I could tell her that she couldn't.

In July, Beach and I took the Abenteurers down Cataract Canyon. The river had dropped. They were bored. Not enough vitevasser, Fritz complained. Beach Philips had an idea to add some excitement. Instead of motoring off the endless lake, we'd hike them up and out Dark Canyon to the Sundance Trail.

The Abenteurers packed their Abenteurer backpacks. Neither Fritz nor Jurgen wanted to make the hike but they sent the team doctor with us. He was about 200 pounds. The weather was over 100. The Team was slow at scrambling and rockhopping. It was hot. Beach and I ran up above the next waterfall and smoked and waited in the shade for them to catch up.

By the time we reached the mesa the Marlboro doctor was wheezing and sweating and had to drop his head between his knees. And Fritz was waiting there for us, leaning against his jeep touching his mustache, suntanned and very satisfied.

When the Abenteurer Team returned in August, Fritz and Jurgen had thought up a new adventure to beat all. The Team would be helicoptered to Hite Marina airstrip, shuttled to the Sundance Trailhead, hiked down Dark Canyon, whisked off the lake in motorboats.

My boss called me into the office and handed me the credit cards. Drive to Lake Powell, rent two boats, tow one up to the mouth of Dark Canyon and pick up the Marlboro boys. He said there were two types of boats to rent. A sixteen-foot skiff with a 25-horsepower outboard and an eighteen-foot speed boat with 125 horses. He wanted me to rent the smaller boat because it was fifty dollars a day. The waterski boat cost 180. I would have to decide when I got there if the aluminum skiffs were big enough for all my Abenteurers.

The tricky part was insurance, he said. You couldn't get insurance to travel upstream past the Hite Bridge to Dark Canyon. There was current from the river and driftwood and debris. It was considered dangerous.

You've run motorboats, he said. I couldn't tell if he meant it as a question. It was peak season and all the qualified people were down the river. I had driven a rubber raft with a two-stroke outboard a few times.

All the time, I said. No problem.

Beach and I left Moab in two company vehicles. I had a jacked up four-wheel-drive Ford Van and Beach was in a 1976 Land Cruiser. We drove out Indian Creek, then up Elk Basin to the Marlboro camp on Cathedral Point. From the buttress pushing out over the Needles you could see hundreds of snaky cracks in the mesa, split by the gorge of the Colorado. It was too deep and twisted to see the river.

In camp was a bonfire and a mess line with beef and beer. Someone in a cowboy hat sang through his nose and plucked a guitar. Jurgen welcomed us and told us tomorrow's plan. We were to get up early.

It rained all night. In the morning, instead of taking the old clay prospecting roads between the Bear's Ears we backtracked to the highway then cut south. We stopped in Blanding for coffee but it tasted bad and I saw Beach dump it out the window on the highway. He pulled over at Fry Canyon Lodge and made me charge some eggs and bacon and hot coffee on the company card. He said the Germans could wait.

We were late to the Hite airstrip and the Abenteurers were already sweating and pink. The helicopter was gone and they were huddled beneath the tin sunshade. We are waiting here forty-five minutes, one of them said. Yeah yeah, said Beach Philips, get in. They got in. We raced over the bridge and turned onto a dirt road.

Dark Canyon carved down from the Abajo Mountains across the mesa. Beach and I had meant to get there early and reconnoiter the trailhead but now we were late and didn't know which way to go. We couldn't find the map but we'd been to the trailhead before. It would be hard to miss.

Beach was racing the Toyota. He sailed over the bumps and his passengers floated up toward the ceiling. My van with nine Abenteurers felt like a plane crash when it hit sandstone so I slowed down. Beach had to wait at the forks. I didn't know where he was leading us. Somehow he found a wide dirt turnaround that turned out to be the trailhead.

The sun was already high and hot and there were no shadows. The mesa was a flat range of red clay and pinyon in every direction. A few square buttes jutted up in the distance. Blue mountain peaks were far off and blurry through the heat. We unloaded the Team and I told them I'd see them at the lake. They hefted on packs and plodded single-file down the trail.

Vee meet at half past tree, said Jurgen with his finger on his mustache. No later.

Beach's job was to hike the Germans down to the lake. It was a steep but easy walk so the Abenteurer Team brought along a rockclimbing guide to make it more of an adventure. They would find a chasm to set a Tyrolean traverse then rappel to the canyon floor and follow the stream to the lake. I'd be waiting there with two boats and we'd motor them back to Hite to their helicopter.

Down at the marina I looked at the rental boats on the docks. The skiff was like what my grandmother used to fish in. I hopped in and it rocked dangerously. There was a plaque riveted to the hull that said the Coast Guard only allowed six people in such a boat. I would have seven.

I moved over to the speed boat. It was deluxe. It had a steering wheel and a windshield, padded vinyl seats and a convertible sun canopy. Whattaya say, said the dockhand. He could see I liked it.

I'll take two.

Next I had to learn to drive it. I signed some forms then putted out past the buoys. My vessel was called the Funseeker. The throttle lever was bound in leather and had the high quality worn feel of a sit-inside video game. I pulled it.

The boat lurched and bucked and as it shot forward I gripped the steering wheel. The speedometer spun to 45. It was fine. I pressed a button and heard a satisfactory whirring noise. The motor cocked outward and the Funseeker floated up on plane. It was sunny and very smooth.

Back at the marina the dockhand eyed me when I said I needed to tow one of my two boats up to Dark Canyon, but gave me a coil of cotton rope anyway. Did I know that there was no insurance up there above the bridge?

It's okay, I said, I'm doing this for my job.

I tied up the boats and sputtered onto the lake. When I gunned it the rope stretched taut like a slingshot. The Funseeker didn't move, but then the rope recoiled and in the moment of slack we shot forward like I was driving a yo-yo. I passed under the highway bridge into a narrow canyon where the lake looked like a river with no current. My boat strained at the bit dragging the other one up the lake. I had a map but all the cliffs looked the same so I just kept going. The twelve miles up to Dark Canyon took three hours.

The lake was high and the canyon mouth was flooded. Willow and tamarisk stalks poked up from underwater. I steered between the reeds in a deep green channel until driftwood and scum blocked the way, then I tied to the cliff and killed the motor. The creek had flashed and it looked like chocolate.

My watch said it was three o'clock and I lay down and slept until the Abenteurers arrived in their Marlboro knapsacks. They sloshed through the muck with brown grime all up their legs.

That's your boat, I said to Beach, and showed him which buttons to push. He turned the key and roared away. He'd never driven one either but he just knew how to do things like this. My passengers loaded in and I took off after him.

At the canyon mouth we throttled up and made a wide turn onto the lake. We raced each other, and Beach Philips took the lead and I cut behind him and launched off his wake and splatted down cockeyed and felt the weight of the Abenteurers rock to one side. I straightened it out and we flew past water and cliffs and sun. The boats were fast and everything was going right.

When we delivered the crew to the airstrip where the helicopter was waiting, Jurgen told us to meet him seven sharp the next day to start over. Same adventure, different Abenteurers. The blades beat the air. The Team loaded up and the chopper sailed away.

Beach Philips and I drove back to the marina and walked out on the floating dock. Out past the houseboat colony, Jet Skis and waterskiers zipped back and forth before the desert cliffs. It was 94 degrees and there were two hours of sunlight left on Lake Powell and we had nothing to get done till the next day.

We gassed up the Funseekers with the credit cards and motored onto the lake. Without any passengers they soared up on plane and I pulled back the throttle as far as it would go. It was fast and smooth and with every turn a sheet of water fanned out behind me and the hot wind gave me tears and spread them across my face. I could feel the molecules evaporate off my eyeballs and I felt a million drops of air jet up my nose and bounce around my skull and spill out my ears and I felt good. After a lap we stopped and dropped our clothes and dove into the clear water, then back on the boats we drove faster, the motor sang and my stomach fell and I bounced on the windwaves and the walls of Glen Canyon blurred in the sun, houseboats were like tin cans in the distance and there was enough gasoline to go forever, and we carved circles and arcs and figure eights naked, charged chicken and veered away, full speed up some canyon I don't know the name of and spun to a stop where the drowned willows poked up, and I breathed out and breathed in and gunned it out of there in the direction we came.

The lake was wide and flat and there was a lot of it to go.

Sources

CHAPTER 2: DOWN HERE IN THE HOBBIT HOLE

Clark, Reino and Wendy. "The Desert Queen Ranch." Joshua Tree Natural History Association, 1975.

Fong-Torres, Ben. *Hickory Wind: The Life and Times of Gram Parsons.* New York: Simon & Schuster, 1991.

Kaufman, Phil. *Road Mangler Deluxe.* Lafayette, Colo.: White-Boucke Publishing, 1995.

Siebecker, Alice. "Mining in Joshua Tree National Monument." Joshua Tree Natural History Association, 1981.

Weight, Lucile. "Brands: Joshua Tree National Monument." Joshua Tree Natural History Association, 1975.

CHAPTER 3: NAVAJO WHITE

Brigham, Robert. "Land Ownership and Occupancy by Negroes in Manhattan Beach, California." Master's thesis, California State University, Fresno, 1956.

CHAPTER 6: A FAIR SPOT FOR A PICNIC

Chavez, Angelico (trans.), and Ted J. Warner (ed.). *The Dominguez-Escalante Journal*. Provo, Utah: Brigham Young University, 1976.

CHAPTER 8: GERMS

Ringholz, Raye C. *Uranium Frenzy*. New York: W. W. Norton, 1989.

CHAPTER 9: MAID OF THE CANYON

Miller, David E. *Hole-in-the-Rock*. Salt Lake City: University of Utah Press, 1959.

Powell, John Wesley. *The Exploration of the Colorado River and Its Canyons*. New York: Dover, 1961.

Rusho, W. L. *Everett Ruess: A Vagabond for Beauty*. Salt Lake City: Peregrine Smith, 1983.

CHAPTER 10: BUTCH CASSIDY DAYS

Baker, Pearl. *The Wild Bunch at Robbers Roost*. Lincoln, Neb.: University of Nebraska, 1989.

Betenson, Lula Parker. *Butch Cassidy, My Brother*. Provo, Utah: Brigham Young University, 1975.

Kelly, Charles. *The Outlaw Trail: A History of Butch Cassidy and His Wild Bunch*. Lincoln, Nebraska: University of Nebraska Press, 1996.

Pointer, Larry. *In Search of Butch Cassidy*. Norman, Neb.: University of Nebraska Press, 1977.

CHAPTER 14: THIS IS THE PLACE

Arrington, Leonard J. *Brigham Young: American Moses*. Urbana, Ill.: University of Illinois, 1985.

Brodie, Fawn M. *No Man Knows My History: The Life of Joseph Smith*. New York: Random House, 1995.

CHAPTER 15: HISTORICAL TOUR AT THE BUTTERFIELD SOUTHERN

Allen, Paul. "Dragoon Springs," *Tucson Citizen*, date unknown.

Arnold, Elliot. *Blood Brother*. Lincoln, Neb.: University of Nebraska Press, 1979.

Howard, Gen. O. O. "The Indians: Account of Gen'l Howard's Mission to the Apaches and Navajos." *Washington Daily Morning Chronicle,* 1872.

Acknowledgments

I want to thank my brother, Richard, for loaning me the computer to write this book on. I plan to return it soon.

I thank Jeffrey Libby for his editing and encouragement, and also Richard Abate, Tim Bluhm, Noel Riley Fitch, Francesca Gabbiani, John Kim, Joshua Kotzin, Rae Meadows, Nancy Morgan, Curtis Noel, Eric Puchner, Tristine Rainer, Richard Reeves, Hubert Selby, Jr., James Taylor, Ann Treistman, Amanda Urban, and Diana Watson. Without them I might not have finished this book.

Most of all I have to thank Erik R. Bluhm. Without him I would not have started.

ABOUT THE AUTHOR

Mark Sundeen was born in 1970 in
Harbor City, California. He is a
contributor to and managing editor
of *Great God Pan* magazine. This is
his first book.